Angel Dreams

Also by Doreen Virtue and Melissa Virtue

Oracle Cards (divination cards and book)

Angel Dreams Oracle Cards

Also by Doreen Virtue

Books/Calendar/Kits/Oracle Board

Angels of Love (with Grant Virtue; available January 2015)

The Survival Guide for Indigos
(with Charles Virtue; available January 2015)

Angel Lady (available November 2014)

The Big Book of Angel Tarot
(with Radleigh Valentine; available July 2014)

Angels of Abundance (with Grant Virtue)

Angel Astrology 101 (with Yasmin Boland)

Angel Detox (with Robert Reeves)

Assertiveness for Earth Angels

How to Heal a Grieving Heart (with James Van Praagh)

The Essential Doreen Virtue Collection

Whispers from Above 2014 Calendar

The Miracles of Archangel Gabriel

Mermaids 101

Flower Therapy (with Robert Reeves)

Mary, Queen of Angels

Saved by an Angel

The Angel Therapy® Handbook

Angel Words (with Grant Virtue)

Archangels 101

The Healing Miracles of Archangel Raphael

The Art of Raw Living Food (with Jenny Ross)

Signs from Above (with Charles Virtue)

The Miracles of Archangel Michael

Angel Numbers 101

Solomon's Angels (a novel)

My Guardian Angel (with Amy Oscar)

Angel Blessings Candle Kit (with Grant Virtue;
includes booklet, CD, journal, etc.)

Thank You, Angels! (children's book with Kristina Tracy)

Healing Words from the Angels

How to Hear Your Angels

Realms of the Earth Angels

Fairies 101

Daily Guidance from Your Angels

Divine Magic

How to Give an Angel Card Reading Kit

Angels 101

Angel Guidance Board

Goddesses & Angels

Crystal Therapy (with Judith Lukomski)

Connecting with Your Angels Kit
(includes booklet, CD, journal, etc.)

Angel Medicine

The Crystal Children

Archangels & Ascended Masters

Earth Angels

Messages from Your Angels

Angel Visions II

Eating in the Light (with Becky Black, M.F.T., R.D.)

The Care and Feeding of Indigo Children

Healing with the Fairies

Angel Visions

Divine Prescriptions

Healing with the Angels

"I'd Change My Life If I Had More Time"

Divine Guidance

Chakra Clearing

Angel Therapy®

The Lightworker's Way

Constant Craving A–Z

Constant Craving

The Yo-Yo Diet Syndrome

Losing Your Pounds of Pain

Audio/CD Programs

The Healing Miracles of Archangel Raphael

Angel Therapy® Meditations

Archangels 101 (abridged audio book)

Fairies 101 (abridged audio book)

Goddesses & Angels (abridged audio book)

Angel Medicine (available as both 1- and 2-CD sets)

Angels among Us (with Michael Toms)

Messages from Your Angels (abridged audio book)

Past-Life Regression with the Angels

Divine Prescriptions

The Romance Angels

Connecting with Your Angels

Manifesting with the Angels

Karma Releasing

Healing Your Appetite, Healing Your Life

Healing with the Angels

Divine Guidance

Chakra Clearing

DVD Program

How to Give an Angel Card Reading

Oracle Cards

Fairy Tarot Cards
(with Radleigh Valentine; available December 2014)

Past Life Oracle Cards
(with Brian Weiss, M.D.; available October 2014)

Guardian Angel Tarot Cards
(with Radleigh Valentine; available August 2014)

Cherub Angel Cards for Children (available June 2014)

Angels of Abundance Tarot Cards (with Radleigh Valentine)

Talking to Heaven Mediumship Cards (with James Van Praagh)

Archangel Power Tarot Cards (with Radleigh Valentine)

Flower Therapy Oracle Cards (with Robert Reeves)

Indigo Angel Oracle Cards (with Charles Virtue)

Mary, Queen of Angels Oracle Cards

Angel Tarot Cards (with Radleigh Valentine and Steve A. Roberts)

The Romance Angels Oracle Cards

Life Purpose Oracle Cards

Archangel Raphael Healing Oracle Cards

Archangel Michael Oracle Cards

Angel Therapy® Oracle Cards

Magical Messages from the Fairies Oracle Cards

Ascended Masters Oracle Cards
Daily Guidance from Your Angels Oracle Cards
Saints & Angels Oracle Cards
Magical Unicorns Oracle Cards
Goddess Guidance Oracle Cards
Archangel Oracle Cards
Magical Mermaids and Dolphins Oracle Cards
Messages from Your Angels Oracle Cards
Healing with the Fairies Oracle Cards
Healing with the Angels Oracle Cards

Also by Melissa Virtue

Books

Magical Dream Journeys: #1 Gena's Underwater Adventure (Virtue Press)
Magical Dream Journeys: #2 The Forest Wizard (Virtue Press)
Magical Dream Journeys: #3 The Book of Secrets (Virtue Press)
Dreamtime (Virtue Press)

Please visit:

Hay House UK: www.hayhouse.co.uk
Hay House USA: www.hayhouse.com®
Hay House Australia: www.hayhouse.com.au
Hay House South Africa: www.hayhouse.co.za
Hay House India: www.hayhouse.co.in

Doreen's website: www.AngelTherapy.com
Melissa's website: www.SacredSolas.com

ANGEL DREAMS

Healing and Guidance
from Your Dreams

Doreen Virtue
and Melissa Virtue

HAY HOUSE

Carlsbad, California • New York City • London • Sydney
Johannesburg • Vancouver • Hong Kong • New Delhi

First published and distributed in the United Kingdom by:
Hay House UK Ltd, Astley House, 33 Notting Hill Gate, London W11 3JQ
Tel: +44 (0)20 3675 2450; Fax: +44 (0)20 3675 2451
www.hayhouse.co.uk

Published and distributed in the United States of America by:
Hay House Inc., PO Box 5100, Carlsbad, CA 92018-5100
Tel: (1) 760 431 7695 or (800) 654 5126
Fax: (1) 760 431 6948 or (800) 650 5115
www.hayhouse.com

Published and distributed in Australia by:
Hay House Australia Ltd, 18/36 Ralph St, Alexandria NSW 2015
Tel: (61) 2 9669 4299; Fax: (61) 2 9669 4144
www.hayhouse.com.au

Published and distributed in the Republic of South Africa by:
Hay House SA (Pty) Ltd, PO Box 990, Witkoppen 2068
Tel/Fax: (27) 11 467 8904
www.hayhouse.co.za

Published and distributed in India by:
Hay House Publishers India, Muskaan Complex, Plot No.3, B-2,
Vasant Kunj, New Delhi 110 070Tel: (91) 11 4176 1620; Fax: (91) 11 4176 1630
www.hayhouse.co.in

Distributed in Canada by:
Raincoast Books, 2440 Viking Way, Richmond, B.C. V6V 1N2 Tel: (1) 604 448
7100; Fax: (1) 604 270 7161; www.raincoast.com

Copyright © 2014 by Doreen Virtue and Melissa Virtue

The moral rights of the authors have been asserted.

Cover and Interior design: Nick C. Welch

The information given in this book should not be treated as a substitute for professional medical advice; always consult a medical practitioner. Any use of information in this book is at the reader's discretion and risk. Neither the authors nor the publisher can be held responsible for any loss, claim or damage arising out of the use, or misuse, of the suggestions made, the failure to take medical advice or for any material on third party websites.

A catalogue record for this book is available from the British Library.

ISBN: 978-1-78180-233-5

Printed and bound in Great Britain by TJ International, Padstow, Cornwall.

To Archangel Michael,
who watches over all of us as we sleep.
— Doreen

To Grant, my heart's dream.
— Melissa

CONTENTS

· * *· ·**· · **·*· *·** *· ·

INTRODUCTION

Dreams are gateways to other worlds, times, and planes of existence. They are sacred spaces in which we receive messages brought to us from Source. When we are sleeping, our conscious mind is pushed out of the way so that we may be more open to this information. Therefore, in dreamtime, we allow ourselves to be conduits for the healing, understanding, and growth we need. When we expand our understanding of our dreams, we receive guidance from Source as to how to achieve our highest good and potential.

A Bit of Dream History

Dreams have been studied and revered for many thousands of years. Ancient peoples built temples specifically for use in dream-related ceremonies. They performed rituals, such as dancing and chanting, for the purpose of dream preparation.

Dreams were also used as oracles in cultures of antiquity. A prophetic dream was manifested to relay important survival information or other messages for the community.

Common among cultures around the world was the practice of holding dreamtime sacred. It was considered a holy art form, a gift from the Great Divine. The ancient people knew that dream messages they received were intended to serve their highest good. They also recognized that each person has a dream guide (a being you will learn more about in Chapter 1).

About This Book

Delivered by a dream guide and oftentimes angels, messages from Source can be symbolic in nature. There are various types of dreams, and each one offers opportunities for awareness, healing, and growth. However, the purpose of this book is sharing and learning about dreams that involve angels. Thus, we will cover only the basics such as flying dreams, healing dreams, and dreams involving passed-over loved ones and animals.

We asked readers to send us their own stories of their heavenly encounters. While dreams are quite personal and each one is unique, we chose a few that best represented the basic types of angel dreams. Our hope is that you, too, will be inspired to open yourself up to receiving guidance in dreamtime from these Divine messengers.

There are two parts to this book: Part I deals with introductory information about dream guides, as well as techniques for dream recall and creation. Part II explores the meaning of common dream symbols (some of which are also found in our previous work, *Angel Dreams Oracle Cards),* and contains explanations of various types of dreams. This also includes example dreams of each type and their general interpretations. (To give a complete detailed interpretation would require more pages than space here allows, as well as a discussion with the dreamer.)

With *Angel Dreams,* we invite you to travel across the threshold to dreamtime—a sacred realm that may involve past, present, or future environments. Welcome to the magical world of dreams!

— **Doreen** and **Melissa**

PART I

ABOUT ANGEL DREAMS

Chapter One

Understanding the Basics

Although ordinary rules do not apply to the world of dreams, through experience, study, and interviewing hundreds of people from around the world, we have discovered certain common parameters. It may be helpful to think of most of these structures as flexible—elastic, like rubber bands—and open to personal interpretation. As we begin to understand and work with them, we can learn how to expand and shift them.

In this chapter, we will explore a few myths about dreams and how to interpret them. We will also explain common factors in dreams, where the images really come from, and how your guides and angels fit into all of this.

The Way We Dream

It may surprise you to learn that everyone dreams every night. However, one of the most common issues is forgetting everything upon awakening. One reason is due to generally feeling stressed or overwhelmed. Or perhaps you set a jarring alarm that jolts you awake. Your dream body then "jumps" back into your physical body, startling your memories away. Learning to decipher your dream messages is one way to aid in recall, and we'll go over more techniques in the next chapter.

Colorful, vivid images are ideal, but there are many people who dream in black-and-white instead. Those who do so tend to suppress their artistic expression, their feelings, and their appetite. They might even feel physically, emotionally, mentally, or spiritually stuck, such as in their jobs, in their relationships, or creatively. It seems the color is drained from their daily life, and thus their dreamtime is also drained of color. Those who express themselves and vocalize their truth tend to have very rich, vibrant dreams.

Another issue affecting our dreamtime is how we feed ourselves. It is very important to nourish our physical bodies with proper, healthy fuel. You cannot jam a bagel into the gas tank of your car and expect it to still run properly! Your body is your sacred vehicle; it needs to be cared for and well maintained.

A balanced diet keeps your body healthy and vibrant, and then your dreams will be, too.

Myths about Dreaming

Have you ever had the following thought: *Oh, I only dreamed about that person because I saw him yesterday?* However, this is not quite true. When you think about it, you see thousands of images every day that don't make their way into your head at night. So it's clear that you do not dream of something just because you saw it that day or the day before.

Instead, what is really happening is that a particular image or person may act as a key that opens the doorway to a certain dream that you need to experience. Your higher self will store this key away until it is needed to convey a message to you in your sleep.

Another common misconception is that some foods trigger nightmares or cause you to dream about certain subjects. While people with healthful eating habits will have more powerful dreams, your choice of food won't lead you to see any particular content. However, you may have poor-quality, restless sleep if you stimulate your system by ingesting spicy food and caffeine, or by watching television right before bedtime. Similarly, sedatives such as alcohol or sleeping pills inhibit the deeply restorative REM sleep cycle, preventing you from having as many dreams as your body requires for optimal health.

When you do have a wild dream, it is because you need to receive its messages, loud and clear. Perhaps you were not paying attention when the information was presented to you before in a gentler manner. Basically, your angels are trying to get your attention. So when you have so-called crazy dreams, it's important to meditate and ask, "What message do you want me to hear?"

Dream Dictionaries and Universal Dream Symbols

While dream dictionaries are readily available, you do not need one to understand your dreams— you are your own best interpreter. In fact, they can misdirect you when you're trying to interpret the images you see. Since a dream dictionary is written from just one author's perspective of what the images symbolize, trusting his or her subjective view can lead you to miss the unique symbolism an image has in the context of your own dreams. For instance, while you might see "passion" in the color red, someone else may associate it with "anger."

As another example, when you think of a bouquet of flowers, you might see a thoughtful, heartfelt, yet temporary gift. Therefore, you would interpret that image as an entreaty to enjoy the moment, for it will soon be gone. However, for another person, fresh blossoms may symbolize romantic love, abundance, or something good about to come into one's life. For yet another person, that bouquet may represent grief, illness, or sadness.

Although the meanings of symbols vary due to the individual significance each image holds for a person, there are certain basic symbols with universal meanings. For example, water is an archetypal symbol that represents emotions or the unconscious. Then, in addition to that general meaning, you can add your own personal meaning. For instance, if you add the adjective *deep* to water (which universally means *emotions*), suddenly water has another meaning —*deep emotions*. Therefore, swimming in deep water would symbolize being deeply emotionally involved in a situation. Then, if you were scared of water, this would add yet another layer of meaning to your dream: being in a deeply frightening emotional situation. However, if water represented enjoyment and paradise to you, deep water could symbolize being in a deeply loving emotional situation.

Always remember that only *you* know what the images you see truly represent. Since your dreams are multilayered, it is important to take time to examine every facet of what something might mean to you when you decode each piece. To help get you started, we provide the general meanings of some common symbols in Chapter 4.

Your Dream Body

Everyone has a dream body. It is sometimes called an astral body, subtle body, or light body, but these terms all mean the same thing. Your dream body melds with your physical body in much the same manner as an aura. It is made up of subtle vibrational energies that are connected to your chakra system and aura. It acts as your energetic vehicle, leaving your physical body sleeping while you explore nonphysical planes in other places and times. The difference is, you feel lighter and you can quite literally fly.

If you were to look at your dream body, instead of skin you would see thousands of tiny stars and universes. You would also notice a silver cord attached at your center, connecting you to the center of your physical body around the belly-button area. This cord acts as your life-support system. It allows you to explore all of the realms, then find your way back. Upon awakening from dreamtime, this attachment helps you reenter your physical body without a problem. It cannot be severed until the end of your life.

Your Dream Guide

We are not left to explore our dreams alone. Since birth, you—like everyone—have had a loving, protective, personal "dream guide," who plays a vital, guardian angel–like role; you might think of your guide as your "dream angel." He or she could be a passed-over loved one, ascended master, angel, archangel, spirit guide, or any being of Divine love and light.

Your guide is with you every night and in every dream, supporting and protecting you. Guides are the gatekeepers to other worlds, and they bring you information that is important for your well-being and highest good. If someone, such as your deceased grandmother, needs to give you a particular message, your guide will allow her into your dream plane. On other occasions this being will act as a bodyguard, evicting lower energies to keep out negativity and nightmares.

Call upon your dream guide for protection and guidance as you're falling asleep, and thank him or her upon awakening.

Angels in Your Dreams

Dreaming of angels can inspire and support you on your journey. It can motivate you toward positive and healthful changes, or be that little nudge of encouragement you needed to keep going. You may dream of a specific angel or simply have the feeling of an angelic presence. In either case, the angel is there in your dreams for the purpose of guiding, protecting, and encouraging you. Upon awakening, you will discover that you feel happier and your heart is filled with warm love.

Archangels may also work in conjunction with your dream guide. Archangels are large, powerful beings who oversee our guardian angels. They are unlimited and nondenominational angels, able to simultaneously help many people. Some archangels offer assistance during your dreams, while others help you prepare for dreamtime. In the following list, the archangels are listed with their dream specialties.

- **Archangel Michael:** protection; standing in your power; problem solving

- **Archangel Raphael:** healing dreams; healing your body during sleep

- **Archangel Raguel:** problem-solving dreams that involve family and friends

- **Archangel Jophiel:** preparing your environment, such as your room or bed, for sleep

- **Archangel Haniel:** opening your third eye; connecting with the moon cycles for dreaming

- **Archangel Gabriel:** bringing prophetic messages

- **Archangel Raziel:** working with you in past-life dreams

- **Archangel Metatron:** cleaning and clearing your dream body in preparation for dream-time

- **Archangel Uriel:** working with problem-solving dreams

Chapter Two

Techniques for Dream
Preparation and Recall

As we've mentioned, everyone dreams every night. Even if you never remember your dreams, there are steps you can take so that you don't lose their messages upon awakening. Along with taking care of your physical body and managing your stress levels, try the following tools and techniques for dream preparation. You can follow the exercises exactly as written, or you can use them as a guide to create your own methods.

Affirmations

An affirmation is a positive statement where you declare that something about yourself is true. It is a form of prayer or intention that focuses on a desirable outcome.

When you say affirmations before you sleep, they set the tone of your night journeys. These statements prime your environment and your energetic vibration as if tuning an instrument for a performance. When you set positive intentions, you give yourself permission to unlock the gateways of understanding and recall the deeper meanings of your dreams.

The following are examples of dream affirmations. Choose one before bed, hold the intention in your mind, and repeat it until you feel the positive energy in your heart.

- *My dreams are always peaceful and healing.*

- *My dreams are for my highest good.*

- *I enjoy dreaming, as it allows me to be more creative.*

- *I carry my dream potential with me into wakefulness.*

- *As I step across the threshold from this world into another, I open myself to magical journeys filled with amazing possibilities.*

Have fun writing your own affirmations!

Your Dream Chamber

Your environment affects your emotional and mental states. Your feelings as you fall asleep influence your mind throughout the night, so it is important to create a calm environment conducive to dreamtime. Think of your bedroom as your personal dream chamber.

Here are some easy tips to consider in preparing your environment:

- Decorate your bedroom using calm blues, greens, and earth tones. This will promote a restful sleep. Include any decorations that make it feel intimate, comfortable, and peaceful—let your room be your haven.

- Be aware of mirrors in your room; they act as gateways for other energies to emerge. Covering your mirrors with beautiful fabrics before bedtime will close off these portals.

- Place a "dream pillow" underneath your pillow. Fill a small sachet with a combination of herbs, flowers, essential oils, and the like, meant to promote sleep or call forth particular dreams. If your dream pillow is filled with the herb mugwort, this will expand your clairvoyant vision and make your dreams incredibly vivid. Including lavender is also helpful for awakening clairvoyance.

- Dedicate a journal and pen to recording your dreams. (We'll elaborate on this later.) Keep them within close reach of your bed.

- Before bed, repeat an affirmation or set your intention for the type of dream and subject you would like to bring forward. Call in your dream guide, as well as any other beings, such as Archangel Michael. (For the most benefits, practice this step every night.)

- Consider making your own dream altar. This sends a message to your subconscious that your dreams are important to you. Your altar will act as a vessel that holds the space in the room sacred. It influences the energy of your environment by setting its vibration to one that is conducive to dreams, like a radio set to the station of dreams. The following are our recommendations for making yours.

Creating Your Dream Altar

Dedicate a small table in your bedroom or a space on your dresser for your dream altar. Even a plain wooden crate works. You can paint it, or decorate it with colorful fabrics and different materials that you like.

Place personal sacred objects upon your altar to infuse its energy with their vibrations. These objects are like seasoning a dish: the spices add nuance to and enhance the flavor, and the special items that you choose for your altar will similarly amplify your dreamtime. You might choose to ornament your altar with beautiful fabrics, interesting materials, oracle cards, dried or fresh flowers, pictures, seashells, crystals, written affirmations, or anything that inspires you.

You can include seasonal or temporary objects with your altar. Perhaps you have a particular situation you want to work on for a while. In that case, you might find an item that represents it and put it on your altar just for a night, or until you feel it is resolved. Then you could replace it with another object or nothing at all.

Experiment! Enjoy adding to, changing, and re-creating your magical altar in your personal dream chamber. Be sure to take a moment to visit your altar and meditate on the objects there before you go to bed each night.

Music

Music taps into our subconscious, influencing our moods, thoughts, and states of being. Check what type of music you are listening to now, or think of the last songs you listened to. What artists and genres are you usually drawn to? What feelings do they produce in you?

Music is important for dream preparation as well. You can listen to anything while getting ready for bed or lying in bed before sleeping. However, it is important not to fall asleep with the television or radio playing. Your subconscious mind will pick up on all that is being said, whether it is positive or not, which will influence your emotions both while sleeping and when you awake.

Therefore, to promote a happy dreamtime, play soothing music before going to bed. You can choose anything that evokes the feelings you wish to carry with you into your dreams. For example, if you want to program yourself for astral travel (more on this in Chapter 9), it would help to play ambient music, music that includes drums, or soundscapes—whatever you associate with galaxies and otherworldly travels. You can play any music, as long as it feels positive and uplifting and elicits the feelings you want in your dreams.

Candle Gazing

In candle gazing, you look at a candle with a focused intention. This is a powerful technique not only for dream work but also for divination, manifestation, and meditation purposes.

To begin, first choose a colored candle. The color promotes a specific energetic vibration, which enhances the types of dreams it represents (see the "Colors" section in Chapter 4). For example, blue corresponds to the fifth chakra; it also symbolizes calm, inner truth, and communication. By choosing blue, we are promoting dreams to help us seek inner truth and communication.

After you have selected a candle, find a comfortable seat, then put the candle somewhere safe (perhaps at your altar) and light the wick. Allow your gaze to soften as you begin focusing on the flame. The fire is transmuting, or "burning away," any energies you need to release before dreamtime. The color of the candle is setting the intention for the types of dreams you would like to journey through.

Beyond the symbolism of the color of your chosen candle, you can also "charge" it with an intention or affirmation. (You can learn more about candle gazing and candle magic in Doreen and Grant Virtue's *Angel Blessings Candle Kit,* which holds a wealth of information.)

Water Magic

It is important to prepare your dream body each night before you go to bed. This preparation will also help bring you back into a full state of awareness as you awaken in the morning. Open your dream body to the magical doorway of dreams with this sweet ritual:

Before going to bed, fill a small glass with water. Hold it with both hands, next to your heart or your solar plexus (in the middle of your rib cage).

State an affirmation such as, "My dreams are vivid." Drink half the water. Place the glass somewhere safe nearby.

In the morning, take the half-full glass of water, and hold it again with both hands to your heart or solar plexus. Repeat another affirmation related to recalling your dreams, such as, "I now remember my dreams in vivid color and detail." Drink the remaining water.

With practice, you will now begin to remember more details of your dreams.

This dream-inducing ritual works! *Why?* you might ask.

The physical body consists mostly of water. It makes up much of our bloodstream and our cells. When you say affirmations while holding the glass, it changes the molecular structure of the water, essentially fusing your statements with it. Drinking the water "fills" your body with your intentions. You awaken your dream body with this easy technique, thus helping you remember your dreams.

Get "Rolling"

Rolling over is a little-known way of recalling your dreams after you wake up. When you sleep, you toss and turn, shifting into different positions throughout the night, and your body stores memories from your dreams in your tissues. Therefore, rolling yourself into various poses when you awaken can release your body memories to help you recall fragments of the dreams you were having while you were in each position.

For example, while you are dreaming, you might roll to your right side. Your body then stores the dreams you have during this time in the muscles there. If you switch to your left side or your back while you are dreaming, your body records memories in those positions, too. Then, when you awaken, you can gently shift in bed, discovering the different feelings and images you were given in your sleep.

For the step-by-step version:

- Upon awakening, gently roll to your right. Lie there a minute or two.
- Then, slowly roll onto your back and lie there for a few minutes.

- Last, roll onto your left side, resting there for a while before getting up to greet the day.

Take your time, and note the various impressions you got while in each position. This is fun detective work!

Journaling

Journaling is one of the best dream-recall techniques—make it a habit! The more you write, the more details you'll remember. Ideally, you will want to journal every day, immediately upon awakening or as soon as you are able. At first, you may not remember much. But as you continue with this habit, you'll be amazed by how much comes back to you.

You will need a new notebook dedicated to recording your dreams; do not use it for any other purpose. You will also need a favorite pen—again, use it only for writing about your dreams. Keep these two objects on your nightstand or another place next to your bed.

When you awaken in the morning, before doing anything else, pick up your pen and write the date in your notebook. Then, write down everything you can remember from your dreamtime, including the environment, people, sounds, actions, events, what you were wearing, emotions, colors, and your feelings upon awakening. If you can remember only the image of a red shoe, write it down! Go into as much detail as you are able. The more you continue to write in your journal, the more details you will begin to recall from your dreams.

Writing the date is helpful so that you will be able to refer back to other dreams and notice any patterns or trends. This is important, as each of your dreams is a thread; woven together, they form a great tapestry that tells a story. Perhaps you will receive a continual message for a few weeks over a series of dreams that are seemingly unrelated . . . that is, until you review your dream journal. You will then see the magical connection right there on the page.

Note: You may have *flashes* throughout the day, which are moments when you remember random bits of a dream. They are dream fragments, like pieces to a puzzle. Anything can cause a flash, including people, places, and events. It would be wise to carry around a small notebook to record the flashes you may have throughout your day. Later, you can record these in your dream journal.

Dream Discussions

Talking to someone upon awakening and sharing the details of your dreams can be a powerful tool. The more you describe what you experienced, the more details you are likely to recall. Choose someone you trust, like a close friend, a family member, or your partner.

These discussions create a sacred bond and can bring people closer together. The dream space is very intimate; opening your heart and being vulnerable with someone will strengthen your connection on so many levels. When you learn more about the symbolism within your dreams, you'll want to explore possible meanings in your discussions, too.

Creating Art

Drawing, sketching, and painting the images and feelings you had in your dreams will open your heart and mind so that you become more receptive to these memories. When you artistically express your dreams, they can become clearer and more powerful. Don't worry about what your art looks like; just go with the flow and enjoy your creativity. You don't have to break out the canvas and easel, either; you can always just sketch in your dream journal.

Chapter Three

CREATING YOUR OWN DREAMS

Once you've learned how to improve your recall of your dreams, the next thing to master is *creating* your own dreams. After practicing the techniques described in this chapter, you'll be able to "program" your dreams for the healing and guidance that you seek. In this way, your sleep becomes an extension of your self-care work.

Lucid Dreaming

One of the most important forms of dreaming is *lucid dreaming.* This is when you are clearly aware that you are dreaming. Everything will seem vivid and real, and your senses will be intensified. You can then influence the events that are taking place or choose to create a completely new reality.

Sometimes you will have an "Aha!" moment or some other trigger to make you conscious of the fact that you are dreaming. The opportunity for transformation, manifestation, and creativity emerges from that moment of realization. When you open your awareness up to how you can create your dream circumstances, you become very good at manifesting in your waking life.

To promote lucid dreaming, it helps to select a "totem," which can be any significant object. You will be using the sight of it to remind you that you are in the dreamtime, so choose one that best reflects that for you. A body part, such as your hand or foot, can be a great totem, since you will most likely see one of these in any type of dream you have. Do not switch to a different totem after you've selected one. The more you work with it, the more of an energetic charge it will gain. Whenever you see the totem in your dreams, it triggers your memory and you become more and more likely to awaken to the fact that you are dreaming.

Once you are aware you are dreaming, you can then begin to create your dream. For example, you may be dreaming you are in room full of people when you would prefer to be in a field blossoming with flowers. You can make the choice to change your environment so you may be in that colorful field. Or, perhaps in the crowded room, you might choose to approach a specific person in order to begin a conversation.

You can explore all of your options and experiences once you realize you are dreaming. Create a different environment, choose to talk with someone, work on a solution to a problem, create a project, or compose music. All of this is possible in lucid dreaming. Remember to be patient with yourself, as it takes a bit of practice to stay in the lucid dream once you awaken to the fact you are dreaming.

It does take some work to promote lucid dreams, yet that is part of the adventure. The following ancient technique is an excellent place to start practicing. In this exercise, your hand is acting as the totem.

The Tibetan Hand Technique

Focus on your hand before bedtime as you repeat this affirmation (or make up your own with the same meaning): "Upon seeing my hand in my dream tonight, I will remember that I am dreaming." Really examine each detail of your hand. Study it so well that you can still clearly visualize it when you close your eyes.

This preparation will send a note to your subconscious mind to bring your hand to your attention during your night journey. Then, when you do see it, it will activate the intention you set to remind you that you are dreaming.

Programming yourself in this way will enhance your lucid-dream abilities and therefore expand your manifestation skills into your waking reality. If you feel it is not working, relax and just keep practicing. It does take a bit of time. Most important, though, have fun!

Dream Incubation

In ancient times, our ancestors used specialized temples to promote dream work. The majority of these temples were constructed for "incubation." This is a technique to help bring forward specific dreams, to obtain more detail in a dream, and to decode and garner more information about a particular message. Traditionally, some Native American medicine men would fast for days to call forth specific dreams. In ancient Greece, the priestesses and priests would enter a dream temple for days or weeks to work on their dreams. Sometimes fresh herbs were scattered around the area, and herbal drinks were ingested, to promote the desired outcome.

You may have a dream—or another situation in your life—that you do not clearly understand. If you desire more information about it, you can incubate it using the following steps:

1. Just before you go to sleep, write down what you would like to focus on during dreamtime. You might ask: "What in my life needs attention?" or "What situation [or feeling] do I need clarified?" You can also state it in the form of an intention, such as "I will dream about the area of my life that needs attention" or "I will have a dream to clarify my feelings about my relationship [or career or whatever you choose]."

2. After you lie down, repeat your statement or question a few times, and visualize the words you wrote down.

3. You might also place a visual symbol nearby, perhaps on a nightstand, representing the situation or dream you would like to focus upon.

4. If you are more of an olfactory person, place in your pillowcase, on your nightstand, or under your pillow some herbs that represent the dream you would like to incubate. For example, rose soothes the emotional state while protecting the dreamer from nightmares. It can also bring dreams of relationships and matters of the heart. Lavender, on the other hand, relaxes the nerves and can aid in opening the third eye, clairvoyance, and promoting prophetic dreams. Mugwort

cleans and prepares the space for dreamtime if you use it as a smudge, or incense. It also aids in vivid dream recall and stimulates lucid dreaming. Dandelion can bring forth problem-solving dreams. Nettle protects the dreamer while stimulating mirror dreams and problem-solving dreams. Apple blossom primes the dream body for astral traveling to ancient places such as Avalon. Hawthorn invokes dreams of the elemental kingdom and nature. Lady's mantle stimulates dreams of healing—on all levels—and inspiration.

5. Each morning, write down in your dream journal everything you remember, including how you felt when you awakened.

Repeat any or all of these steps to receive the desired results. You may incubate for a few days, for a few weeks, or even for a month, depending on how much information you and your guides feel you need. Be patient and relax while using this technique, as it can take some time.

Incubating a Place

You can also incubate a dream where you travel to sacred places. Certain locations are powerfully charged with energy and electromagnetic currents.

When you think about these places, you become connected to their energy. For example, if you were to look at a picture of Newgrange (an ancient monument in Ireland) for five minutes every day, you would be "dialing" it as if ringing it up on the phone. Newgrange would, of course, answer and connect you to its energy. This is how it works with incubating any sacred or powerful places.

This technique can also work with familiar locations, such as your childhood home, school, or anyplace that feels important or special to you. It can even be somewhere you don't particularly like; it just needs to be a spot that is personally meaningful for you. Unlike sacred places, which hold charges for everyone, personal places hold the charge only for whoever has had a personal experience with the space.

The technique is simple: Look at a picture of a sacred (or personal) place just before bedtime or while you are lying in bed. Focus on it for five minutes or more. Then close your eyes, and see the picture in your mind's eye. You have now dialed the sacred place. As you drift off to sleep, know that the connection is being made to this locale.

•★•

You can incubate dreams for as long as you like. When your dream guide and angels feel you need to focus on other messages that would better serve you, they will lead you there. Remember, you will always receive that which is for your highest good, even if it's not the particular experience you thought you were seeking. Enjoy this fascinating journey.

Awake Dreaming

Just as it is possible to create your nightly dreams, you can also use manifestation in your waking life. *Awake dreaming* (also known as *daydreaming*) is a sweet manner in which to relax and discover your hidden creativity and potential. Many best-selling books, top movies, award-winning plays, and other works of art have been inspired by awake dreaming.

It's said that Mark Twain, Mozart, Beethoven, Albert Einstein, and Isaac Newton all received new ideas while daydreaming. Thomas Edison's teacher complained that he was "prone to daydream" during class. Arthur Fry, a 3M engineer, was looking for a way to keep bookmarks from falling out of his choir book, and one day, while his mind was wandering, he remembered a colleague who had a special glue. He put the results of his daydream into immediate practice by inventing the Post-it.

Scientific studies using MRI scans show that the brain activity associated with complex problem solving is more active during daydreams. Other research has concluded that students who regularly daydream have more empathy. Perhaps it's because it awakens our intuition, which is related to empathy. A 2010 Harvard study estimated that people are daydreaming about something other than their present activity about 47 percent of the time.

As you relax and permit your mind to wander, your consciousness relaxes, too. This allows visions to surface in your imagination like a movie. Some call this "stream of consciousness." If you allow yourself to be at ease in this "zone," you can be inspired by all kinds of new ideas, and projects will pop into your head through this stream of thought from your creative mind.

For example, Eric was a choreographer who was asked to create a dance for a famous television awards ceremony. He was a bit stressed trying to come up with ideas. There was always an element missing, and nothing felt right. So, after weeks of work, he decided to take a break at a coffee shop.

As Eric relaxed, his mind began to wander, leading him into a free flow of visions, thoughts, and ideas. He allowed himself to stay in this zone, and an inspiring string of images began to form in his mind. Almost in a trance, he picked up his pencil and wrote down everything he saw as it came: costumes, dance steps, music, themes. It was as if he were channeling or performing automatic writing. He saw the images clearly as each one merged into the other. After a few hours, the stream began to taper off, and Eric knew he had his choreography. This awake dream bore fruit as his first widely acclaimed work.

Sometimes awake dreaming happens when you least expect it. Pay attention to the information that arises. You can use the following technique to help with opening yourself up to awake dreams.

- Allow your body and mind to relax.

- Soften your gaze, so that it's not focused upon anything in particular.

- Call upon your dream guide and anyone else who can help you, such as an archangel, ascended master, or spirit guide.

- As images begin to flow into your mind, allow your thoughts to wander freely.

- You might want to ask a question. Write down the message you receive. You will probably receive an answer through visuals, such as colors and symbols.

- Continue to ask questions, or simply allow whatever visions you have formed to flow easily.

- After the images have dissipated, write them down in your journal. Our angels and spirit guides urge us to take time to daydream, as we often receive Divine messages through them.

PART II

INTERPRETING
YOUR DREAMS

Chapter Four

Basic Dream Symbols

In this chapter, we offer a list of common symbols and what they generally represent. However, it is up to you to fully assimilate the images and feelings that you get in your dreams. Remember, you are your own best dream interpreter. Only the dreamer can understand the true meaning.

As you read, check in with how you resonate with each symbol. Consider what personal significance it might have for you if you saw it in the dreamtime.

Angels

Spiritual messages. When you see these messengers of God in your dream, you are truly visiting with them. They are supporting you in your goals for your highest good. Pay attention to what they look like, what they say, and how you feel when you are around them.

Animals

When dreaming of animals or insects, take note of the specific type. Research its habitat and other characteristics. This information may help you understand why you have dreamed of this particular creature.

Bear

Protection, hibernation, mothering. This animal may signal that you need to protect yourself by drawing boundaries. It can also indicate a need to "hibernate," or draw your energies inward to rest and nourish yourself. Alternatively, it might be saying that you need to come out of hibernation and enjoy life.

The bear also represents the mothering quality and abilities in all people. If you see this animal in your dreams, a loved one may need your help, or it may be time to nurture yourself. Consider, too, whether you are being too smothering to someone in your care.

Bird

Freedom, flight, hope. This is the messenger of the angels, spirits, and Source. When birds show up in your dreams, they are bringing you information to help you raise your awareness. They are linking your physical realm to the heavens, and your waking life with dreaming.

Although birds can be a portent of things to come, they are always messengers of hope. If you notice the species of bird, look it up when you awaken; this will add another layer of meaning to its message.

Snake

Integration, release, rebirth. The snake heralds a time of transition, during which you will go through the cycle of birth, death, and rebirth. Enjoy the shedding of the old while stepping into your power.

The snake's wisdom may lead you to ask yourself many questions: *What project or relationship do I need to begin? What do I need to shed, release, or uncover in order to bring about new opportunities? What do I need to bring back into my life?* The snake represents rebirth in all forms. It symbolizes hidden teachings or information, as well as the integration of the physical and spiritual form.

The double snake, or *caduceus*, is the emissary of transcendence—a balance between your physical and spiritual energies. (You might recognize the caduceus as the traditional medical insignia.) Open your awareness to the spiraling dance of cosmic forces symbolized by the two snakes winding around the staff. Study the hidden knowledge that has been beckoning you.

Blood

Life-force energy. If you or someone else is bleeding in a dream, this symbolizes the loss of life-force energy in a particular situation or relationship. An injury without bleeding denotes that while the situation may cause a small amount of mental, physical, or emotional hurt, you will recover with your life-force energy intact.

Clothes

Self-expression, feelings, outward expression. Clothes represent your inner feelings and how you express yourself through what you show to the world. The phrase *wearing your feelings* comes to mind. Clothes can represent both your inner and outer feelings and identity. You'll have to discern what your dream is telling you through the clothing's details. If your clothes are too tight, perhaps your environment or situation no longer fits you. If you dream of dressing well and being complimented on your fabulous appearance, yet you feel very uncomfortable, this may be a sign that you are not being honest in what you are presenting to others. The colors of your clothing add another dimension of meaning (see next entry).

Colors

The meaning of colors is based on the chakra system. When interpreting a color in your dream, as with any symbol, first consider the general meaning, then add your personal feelings about it. While dreaming, take note of any colors that stand out to you, such as in clothing, animals, or physical features. Also, keep an eye out for anything that possesses an unusual coloring. (An object such as the sky, sun, moon, or anything with its normal coloring probably does not need to be analyzed.)

Red

Root chakra, passion, survival instincts, sexual energy. Red is associated with the first (root) chakra. It pertains to your physical body at its deepest levels, and it shows up in dreamtime to let you know whether you are balanced or unbalanced, grounded or scattered. This color asks you to trust that your instincts are sound and will warn you away from harm, if necessary.

Dreaming of this color could also denote that it's time to tune in to your animal impulses, and to discover or acknowledge your passions. Red also represents the circulatory system and the strengthening of life force; perhaps you need to check your blood pressure or your metabolism levels.

Orange

Sacral chakra, creative expression, social sphere, confidence. Orange resonates with the second (sacral) chakra, which is related to the energy of optimism and confidence; change; the social sphere, such as family and society; and creative expression, such as singing and dancing. This color represents the expression of your creativity. It can denote that it's time to discover your hidden talents, make positive changes in your life, or explore pleasurable activities.

Perhaps your experience of pleasure is imbalanced. This is usually manifested in your life as jealousy of another's joy or through losing yourself in drugs, alcohol, food, or sex. In this case, dreaming of this color would be a sign to balance yourself via creative outlets and allow yourself to appreciate beauty.

Dreaming of orange may be a calling for you to let go of your judgments and free your sensuality. Fully awaken to this moment of sensations and emotions, and allow yourself to feel desirable. Transform the mundane into something special. By doing so, you open up a whole new perspective on your daily life. Enjoy your journey.

Yellow

Solar-plexus chakra, flexibility, adaptability, personal power. Yellow represents the third (solar-plexus) chakra. This color pertains to boundaries, so be sure to define yours if you see yellow in your dreams. It also represents the need to identify what is important to you with regard to principles and ethics; you might need to use discernment in your present circumstances.

Consider whether you are being flexible enough in a particular situation, as this color symbolizes being adaptable to change. It can also signal a time to be assertive and allow yourself to be an individual within a group. Perhaps you need to stand up for something you believe in.

Dreaming of yellow might also be revealing an imbalance in your third chakra. Feeling highly competitive with someone else is a sign of this imbalance. You may also feel defensive or insecure, or have conflicts with others.

Green

Heart chakra, compassion, unconditional love, growth, health. This color is associated with the fourth (heart) chakra, which in turn represents healing, growth, love, and nurturing. When green shows up in your dream, it's time to ask yourself what needs healing in your life.

Green also signifies your need to keep your heart open, to be compassionate toward yourself and others, and to allow love to expand your senses. It might be asking you to open up to self-love now and cultivate a relationship with yourself. Green also represents communicating from the heart.

If you're unbalanced in your heart chakra, this color might mean that you need to be employing compassion rather than the energy-depleting emotions of empathy or sympathy. Dreaming of green could be symbolizing the need to allow yourself to receive. Foster a safe and supportive environment by releasing judgment.

Blue

Throat chakra, inner truth, emotional calmness, creative expression, communication. Blue is connected to the fifth (throat) chakra. Perhaps you need to communicate who you are and to accept your originality and uniqueness. This color symbolizes that it's time to jump into your creative expression and to vocalize your thoughts, concerns, or intentions.

Dreaming of this color may be a sign of an imbalance in an area. For example, it might represent your inner truth being stifled. A hint that this is the case is if you feel compelled to prove your views are right. Another clue would be the inability to share your thoughts and opinions, or harboring feelings of inadequacy.

Blue symbolizes the merging of your individual consciousness with the universal consciousness. It can also denote the continuation of learning, such as exploring the beauty in all the world's religions and philosophies. It is an encouragement to stay open to the many pathways of life.

Purple

Third-eye chakra, clairvoyance, royalty. Purple is related to the third-eye chakra. This color might be a signal to you in dreamtime that your third eye is open, and that it's time to use your clairvoyance for the highest good of all. When this chakra is unbalanced, it manifests in the form of a need to escape from reality. If you have feelings of superiority, purple is a reminder that everyone has the same potential, and all people have innate powers of clairvoyance.

Purple has been considered a royal color since ancient times, and dreaming of it can symbolize your connection to royalty or that it's time to give the royal treatment to yourself or someone else. This color also represents that the loving messages you are receiving are Divine, and they're being sent from God, the angels, and your dream guide.

White

Crown chakra, purification, transformation, Source, Divinity, enlightenment. White is the color that reflects all colors. It represents the crown chakra and symbolizes purification, transformation, and Source. Dreaming of white is a reminder of the Divinity within you. When this color shows up in your dreams, it can symbolize that you have all you will ever need inside of you. It is a reminder that you are a spark from Divine Source, a child of Divine love and light.

White might be asking you to surrender to Divine guidance, which is bringing you small glimpses of understanding called enlightenment. You have support in leading a life of sacred awareness; begin by treating all things as holy and worthy of respect.

Death

Transition, life-changing event. Rarely does this symbol mean literal, physical death. When it does, it is usually during a past-life dream or a prophetic dream. However, prophetic dreams of death are rare. Instead, death in dreamtime usually symbolizes a huge transition in one's life, such as a milestone event, or rite of passage. Death also represents the releasing of the old in the form of beliefs, possessions, situations, or relationships that no longer serve you.

Fire

Transmutation, purification, renewal, passion. Fire represents transmutation—having the courage to burn off the old, allowing the new to enter. In other words, it's time to come out of your cocoon and allow yourself to be that beautiful butterfly. It's time to light that inner fire (or the one under your seat!). You know what needs to be done, so get busy and take the steps necessary to allow this wonderful change to occur. Have faith during this time of transition that all is well.

Dreaming of fire also represents purification. In every transformation, a cleansing process takes place. Perhaps it is time to purify your thoughts, actions, relationships, or something else that has become unhealthy. Transmute your old habits.

Hair

Personal power, connection to Source, identification. Since your hair grows from the top of your head, through the crown chakra, it symbolizes the growth or health of your spiritual connection. Hair can also symbolize personal power or a power source. If you dream of your hair being shaved or cut in an unusual style, perhaps you need to explore your roots or a culture that this particular hairstyle reminds you of. This could also symbolize a need for self-identification at this time in your life. Take note of the color of your hair in a dream; if it doesn't match your current color, there may be another layer of meaning.

House

Mind, body, spirit. Just as a house can have many rooms and levels, so do you (physically, mentally, emotionally, and spiritually). When dreaming of a house, take note of how the structure is built. Notice if it is sturdy and what materials it is constructed from. The house reflects your feelings about yourself and your behavior.

Mountain

Attaining goals, higher learning, knowledge, apex, High Council, strength, obstacle, protection. Mountains give you perspective when standing at the peak. Therefore, this can symbolize the need to gain a higher vantage point on a situation. If you dream you're standing at the base of a mountain, this could symbolize a steady climb to reach a goal. The environment of the mountain is also important to note, such as snow, trees, and other such features, as they add to the meaning. Sometimes, dreaming of a mountain symbolizes reaching a higher state of being or learning. Therefore, a mountain can also represent the High Council.

Teeth

Nourishment, verbalization of one's truth and self-expression, control. Teeth are necessary for feeding, as well as communication. If your teeth are falling out or crumbling in a dream, perhaps you feel you are losing control of your voice and unable to express yourself or communicate with someone. If your teeth are crooked, yellowing, or need dental work in your dream, perhaps you need nourishment—mentally, physically, emotionally, or spiritually.

Toilet

Releasing, letting go. Dreaming of this symbol can represent your needing to release something that no longer serves you. It could also mean you need to "flush" a habit. Perhaps you are dumping all of your issues on someone else or they are releasing theirs onto you. If you are using the toilet in a public area or in front of others, this may mean you are feeling emotionally vulnerable, as if you are displaying your emotions to the world.

Tornado

Upheaval. A situation is brewing around you. There will be a cycle of upheaval, then calmness and upheaval again. Be prepared. A tornado can also represent creativity whirling through your life. This creative situation could bring much change.

Traveling

Journey, path, location. If traveling is a theme in your dream, it signals a journey, a new path, or a change in location. Do you know where you're going or where you *want* to go? It is time to make that decision. A shift in geography is coming. Perhaps it's a job relocation or new home.

Reassess your "modes of transportation." Pay attention to how you're piloting your life right now. In what manner are you getting yourself from point A to point B? The vehicle in your dream can represent your physical body, manners, habits, and actions. Take note of who is with you on this journey. Are you in charge of the direction in which you're traveling, or is someone else driving? Reevaluate your choices on your journey at this moment.

Water

Emotion, initiation, rejuvenation. When you see this image, know that you need to tune in to your emotions. Water symbolizes human consciousness. Are you swimming in deep or shallow emotion? Are your feelings muddy or clear? Do they run vast like an ocean? Perhaps it's as if your emotions come crashing down upon you. It is important for you to take time to understand them and their root.

When crossing the threshold of dreamtime, you have the opportunity to explore symbols, messages, and lessons of growth. There is a reason for each dream you experience. You may need the information, awareness, or healing of a particular situation in your life. Knowing the different types of dreams you can have will help you decipher what message you are meant to receive.

Now that we've gone over some of the common dream symbols, we'll describe the various types of dreams, how to recognize them, and what they mean for you. We will also be sharing many examples of each kind of dream from our readers, and giving interpretations so that you can see the many meanings different symbols can have.

Chapter Five

PROBLEM-SOLVING DREAMS

Problem-solving dreams help you understand something in your life that requires attention. When a situation needs to be resolved, your higher self, along with your angels and guides, will bring a problem-solving dream to you. You can analyze the components of these dreams to learn some of or all the following information: the truth of the matter, how you feel in the situation, and how to confront the issue in question. Problem-solving dreams can answer questions like, "What step should I take next?"

In this chapter, we offer examples of problem-solving dreams that readers have shared with us, and how the dreams helped them. If you need more information on how to resolve your own situation, call upon your angels and dream guide to lead you through a problem-solving dream.

Guidance on Your Life's Path

When people are having difficulty navigating issues, or are unsure of what direction their lives should take, the angels might offer guidance, advice, and other support in a dream.

Hazel dreamed that Archangels Michael and Gabriel were guiding her vehicle through a maze-like roundabout. The archangels held mini-suitcases in their hands, and clutched in Gabriel's left hand was a child. Smiling, Gabriel instructed Hazel to guide the child, her niece. Hazel eventually made it through the maze, only to find that she still needed to go around a cliff, taking a mountain road that wound through a jungle.

In this dream, Archangels Gabriel and Michael were showing Hazel that there were some confusing situations coming up in her life, but that they would show her how to find her way through them. The luggage that the archangels held represented Hazel's issues; they were helping carry her burdens.

Hazel felt stuck in the same old routines in her life, and this was reflected in her driving through the maze-like roundabout. The path winding around a cliff, over a mountain, and through a jungle was a sign that, while there would be many obstacles in Hazel's way, she needed to take a risk, depend on her faith, and employ her creativity. The archangels were supporting her, and all she needed to do was ask for help, take a risk, and go for her desire.

And, as it turned out, Hazel's niece really did need her guidance!

．★．

Renée dreamed she was on a bus traveling on a steep, perilous road along a cliff by the sea. She knew by the road conditions that the passengers on the crowded bus were not going to make it. She began to panic until she remembered that the angels offer assistance to anyone who asks them for aid. As she began to call out for help, the bus plummeted into the water below. Renée thought that the angels had abandoned her, and that they hadn't heard her call. She felt sure that she was going to die in the black depths of the ocean.

Just as she was certain of her demise, Renée became aware of a presence. The water was no longer black, but shining like a rainbow. As she looked around, she discovered her guardian angel had come to retrieve her. This vibrant, beautiful being pulled Renée from the depths, and they flew up together through the night sky. Up among the stars, another angel awaited them who appeared to be overseeing the rescue mission. Renée realized these two were her guardian angels; they were always with her and would always hear her call.

The dangerous road Renée was traveling in her dream represented the harmful path she was then taking in her life. The passengers on the bus shared the same plight, showing Renée that she was surrounding herself with people who were all making harmful choices for themselves; if she didn't change, she would share in their tragic fate. The black ocean represented Renée taking a deep emotional plunge into a void. This dream was a reminder to Renée to always ask for help from the angels, and to be open to receiving the help she needed in order to change her life path. Even if it feels like it's too late, if you ask for assistance, the angels do hear you, and life will take a turn for the better.

Cheryl Ann Savoy dreamed that she was being pulled through a portal and found herself whooshed into the middle of a rushing river. It was difficult to see through the pitch-black night, and the water was up to her armpits; she knew she had to get to safety up on the banks. After struggling across the wide river, she found a stone wall at the river's boundaries, with the top just above the reach of her arms. Gathering all her strength and determination, she lunged and hauled herself over the wall and out of the water.

Beyond the river, Cheryl Ann found a thick forest. As she walked through it, she came across a lighthouse, which she instinctively entered. She climbed the staircase into a large room. No one was in the room, but it seemed to belong to an artist. Easels were scattered everywhere with various paints and supplies. Then, through the doorway, a cranky-looking old man entered. Cheryl Ann assumed he was the artist and told him that she must have conjured him. He looked at her quizzically and informed her that she must be mistaken: *he* had conjured *her* up.

It was then that Cheryl Ann noticed a tall, beautiful blond man standing in the room. He was wearing a white cashmere trench coat and had bare feet. She felt his warmth and loving presence, and it dawned on her that he was an angel. Cheryl Ann felt blessed.

Cheryl Ann's dream was telling her to return to her artistic roots and express herself creatively once again. The dark night represented her need to go within to discover the hidden parts of herself that were lying dormant. Rushing rivers can symbolize emotional upheaval, and the stone wall meant that Cheryl Ann had built defenses around her inner turmoil. However, her actions in her dream showed that she had the strength to get over the wall of her emotional defenses.

The lush forest represents that when she overcomes her barriers, she will ground herself and become balanced in her life. The forest also represents the path to growth, and the lighthouse was a beacon calling for Cheryl Ann's attention. As the lighthouse was filled with the artist's supplies, it was a reflection of her need to continue to express herself creatively. The cranky old man was a representation of her emotional self and how she felt about herself for not expressing her art.

• ★ •

John was dreaming that he was in a van with a friend. John's friend was driving dangerously fast; they drove into a large playground overgrown with tall grass and trees, and the van missed hitting the trees by inches. John's friend told him that the city council was not tending to the playground because they did not care about the children. The council just wanted to sell the playground to make a profit.

They then drove to another part of the playground. Standing among a herd of cows was a man dressed in white. The man waved at John with his left hand, while his right hand rested on his heart. When the man waved, a beautiful light emanated from his hand. He knew this man was very special. John noticed that there were four figures standing by the man and waved at them. He was very interested in who this man and the beings were.

John then realized that he was no longer in the van; instead, he was at a spring filling a large bottle of water, and the beautiful man was walking up to him. Offering the man water, John said, "Hello, friend. Would you and your friends like a drink?" The man told John that there was no one with him. At that moment, John realized he was talking to Jesus, and the four beings had been angels.

John was buzzing with energy for days after this dream. The angels knew that John needed a lift in his vitality and spirits. Jesus and the angels were showing John that he needed to slow down to see the important events happening around him, such as the symbolism of the park being sold. John's dream was telling him that Jesus and the angels support him in making some environmental changes for the betterment of children. He considered joining a group that protects children's rights or that brings fresh water to children in the developing world.

Liam felt stuck in his career, yet he felt there were no opportunities to change his path. He decided that although he didn't like many aspects of his professional life, including his co-workers, it was a good job. Then Liam was sent a dream that changed his mind.

Liam dreamed he was holding his high-school diploma and standing on a path in a college campus. In front of him was a fork in the road, and Liam could not decide which path to take. The path to the left looked like spring: there were blooming flowers, birds flitting about, and people riding bicycles. The path to the right looked like it was caught deep in winter: snow blanketed the ground, branches were barren, and few people walked about. Liam felt so drawn to the path of spring. As he began walking along, joy warmed his heart. He even began to skip a bit. Upon awakening, Liam realized what he must do.

It is easy to see in Liam's dream that the winter path represented his current career situation. Winter represents a time for incubation, letting go of the old, dying off, and hibernation. This path felt cold and depressing to Liam, and he knew it was time to release his hold on it.

The lively and colorful spring path excited Liam, and he was happy to be taking this path. Spring symbolizes the blossoming of new ideas, projects, and opportunities. Liam holding his diploma was symbolic of him "graduating" from a lesson. He'd learned it, and now it was time to move forward. The college grounds represented this time of new lessons and forward progression.

Liam was ready for a change, to spread his wings and try new opportunities. His dream showed him that he could stay on the old path and hibernate or try a new one and blossom.

A Helping Hand from the Angels

Angel dreams are vivid and powerful. Sometimes, Source uses them to send a specific message to help us out in a troublesome situation.

Jacqueline remembers her angel dream from 1982. She had just paid a deposit to her divorce lawyer, even though money was not abundant, because she needed closure in this chapter of her life. Jacqueline was very worried when she received a letter from her lawyer stating that her deposit would be forfeit if his balance was not paid within the week.

That night, Jacqueline dreamed that she awakened from her sleep. Standing by the window was a beautiful lady wearing a free-flowing light-blue gown. Jacqueline was in awe of the beauty the lady radiated.

The lady turned to look at Jacqueline and began to speak—but when she opened her mouth, all Jacqueline could hear was the wind. She asked the woman to repeat herself over and over again, but she could not hear a word she said. Then Jacqueline realized that the wind was coming not from the lady but from *her.*

Suddenly, Jacqueline awakened for real. She was saddened and very disappointed because she knew the lady had a message for her. Jacqueline felt she'd awakened before she could figure it out, and she thought about the seemingly missed message all day. Near the end of the day, she got the distinct sense that the lady had been telling her to play a lottery number that she played two weeks ago. Jacqueline very rarely played the lottery, but she felt a hunch about this number, so she thought she would pay attention to it. Jacqueline decided to play the number that very day—and she won! She had almost the exact amount of money she needed to pay off her lawyer, with just $5 to spare.

We know that the lady from Jacqueline's dream was her guardian angel or her dream guide because she was trying to give Jacqueline a message that would be for her highest good. Wind or air, such as what Jacqueline was hearing, represents creativity, new beginnings, fresh ideas, and inspiration. Jacqueline realized that the source of the sound of the wind was coming from *her,* which was a signal that the means for her to start a new beginning would come from inspiration inside herself. Jacqueline discovered a new idea as it came to her in the form of the thought of purchasing a lottery ticket. Winning the money was a new beginning for her, which allowed her to continue the process with her lawyer to receive her divorce and start afresh.

* ★ *

As Carla Jernigan discovered, angels can send very specific information, offering solutions to problems that dreamers do not even realize they have. If your dream guide and angels feel you need information, they will find a way to give it to you. Sometimes, they choose to be direct, as in Carla's dream, where she was literally being visited by the angels.

In her dream, Carla saw silhouettes out of the corner of her eye that looked like human figures, lined up in an array of glowing colors. While they didn't have wings or look like traditional depictions on holiday cards or in movies, Carla realized that they were angels. Their voices sounded like soft echoes as they discussed different plants, flowers, herbs, and scents.

Carla realized she was supposed to be listening to what the beings were saying, but as she focused her attention on them, she felt herself being drawn out of the dream. Before she completely awakened, Carla heard an angel speak very loudly and directly to her: "Never wake up without the smell of juniper."

Carla tried to go back to sleep to get more information, but to no avail. The message was so loud and clear that she could not ignore it, and she decided to take action right away that morning. She jumped out of bed, dressed, and went directly to an herb shop to purchase juniper essential oil. When she returned home, she researched the meaning of juniper and found the information to be relevant to her. Juniper symbolizes protection and fertility and also aids in purification and clairvoyance. Perhaps the angels were telling Carla that she needed to open to her clairvoyance or purify her mind before her day began.

Carla felt she was already on a path of purpose, enlightenment, and joy. Now, however, smelling juniper every morning, she has been put into high gear. She is so grateful for this angel dream!

Nancy Gravel dreamed that she was in a cavern with gigantic quartz crystals jutting out of the soil. Looking up, she saw an illuminated and magnificent being who told her that he was Archangel Uriel. He said that he was her special guardian who accompanied her every day.

Archangel Uriel gave Nancy the message that the quartz were hers. The crystals then began talking to her, telling her that they have a special meaning in her life and trying to impart their messages. Upon awakening, Nancy continued to feel a deep connection to Archangel Uriel.

As in the previous story with the message of juniper, this dream was very clear in its directions. Archangel Uriel and even the crystals were communicating to Nancy loud and clear to begin now, without delay, to incorporate crystals in her life. Doing so has brought many unexpected blessings, and the presence of Archangel Uriel in Nancy's dream has brought peace to her soul.

Healing with the Angels

Dreams aren't an avenue solely for receiving messages and reassurance from the angels. Angels sometimes use them to offer assistance through therapeutic advice and even physical healing. When Jennifer and her husband desperately needed aid for their daughter, they did not expect their prayers to be answered through a dream.

In the summer of 2010, their daughter was born, perfect in all ways. Three months later, however, the little girl began having seizures and developed frightening breast lumps. They called the doctor immediately and were informed that their daughter had a very large, possibly cancerous cyst. Jennifer immediately began praying for a cure. She held on to her faith that her daughter would be taken care of.

One night Jennifer dreamed of a beautiful angel surrounding her daughter in healing light. The next day, during a medical evaluation, the doctors informed her and her husband that the cyst had shrunk! Surgery would no longer be necessary until they could find the cause.

Then, in 2012, the cyst started growing again. Jennifer was frightened, but she continued to pray. Just as had happened before, Jennifer had a dream of angels with her daughter. She saw four heavenly beings passing her little girl around and playing with her as she laughed with joy. When Jennifer awoke, she found her daughter giggling as she slept.

After more evaluations, Jennifer was incredibly relieved to discover that the cyst was entirely gone— and it has not returned! Jennifer now firmly believes in the power of healing dreams.

Dress-Rehearsal Dreams

During dress-rehearsal dreams, the angels walk you through all the options you have at any given moment to help you solve the dilemma you're facing. You will delve to your root feelings to discover the inner truths you may be ignoring when you're awake. When you're trying to make a decision, these types of dreams can help you figure out your course of action. Sometimes, you will be sent this type of dream even when you aren't conscious that there is a decision you need to make, yet afterward you'll be able to make a choice to change your life for the better. You will clearly know which path to take upon awakening from a dress-rehearsal dream.

Think of yourself as a dancer preparing for a performance. You know the steps, the musical cues, and the direction in which you enter and exit the stage. You know how to dance with your partner and how all the lifts are supposed to work. Yet you haven't rehearsed in costume with your partner, onstage with all the lights and the set in place, so you don't have a clear feeling of what this dance will be like when all of its elements are present. Therefore, you have a dress rehearsal to see if all elements work together in harmony: you check that your costume fits well; you check your lighting to make sure you can see and be seen properly; and you check that you and your partner are in sync. Basically, you are working out the kinks, making certain you want to go through with the performance as it stands.

It is the same with dress-rehearsal dreams: you are making sure you want to go through with your present choices. Sometimes, during the rehearsal, dancers will decide that something isn't quite right and will want to change what they'd decided on. They try out new steps to see what works better. In the same way, you can change your present path by trying out new options in dreamtime to see what works best for you.

* ★ *

Ellen had been in a relationship with Brian for seven years. She really wanted to get married but was having doubts about whether he was the right man to spend the rest of her life with. However, she felt embarrassed that she could even question a relationship that she had stayed in for so long. Shoving the doubts away, she went about her daily business.

One night, Ellen dreamed of a wedding—*her* wedding. She was waiting near the entrance to the chapel, preparing to walk down the aisle. The pews were crowded with people, but she didn't know any of them. When she looked down at her dress, she was appalled. It was slightly yellow and old, and she hated its old-fashioned style with a restrictive collar that buttoned up to her neck.

Ellen began to notice other details about the wedding that she disliked or that didn't fit her. On top of it all, her fiancé was late, too! In fact, when she realized that her fiancé in the dream was Brian, she broke out in a sweat.

Ellen began to panic. There wasn't a single aspect to this wedding that she loved, so she quickly began looking for the exit. When she spotted the door, Ellen felt a cool breeze brush her face. It felt refreshing and alive, like freedom. She could see the colorful flowers and vibrant land just beyond the exit. She knew she could run outside and escape this ceremony, if she desired. Her other choice was to stay and be stifled, stuck in a commitment she no longer wanted.

Upon awakening, Ellen realized that the feelings the dress-rehearsal dream had brought up were genuine. She knew she wasn't happy and didn't want to commit to the person she was with. She clearly saw the two choices laid before her, and understood on a much deeper level how her heart yearned to release her current relationship. She needed freedom, and she could no longer push aside her feelings or her truth. She needed to take action. When dress-rehearsal dreams show up, they are telling us that the time to make a choice or change a pattern is *now*.

Recurring Dreams

Recurring dreams (ones that you have repeatedly each night) are meant to heal or resolve an issue you have been putting off for too long. When a past hurt or traumatic situation hasn't been resolved, you will tend to have the same dreams until you are healed. They often show up when you have a pattern in your life that's detrimental to your growth. Perhaps you have been ignoring the issue or feel unable to do the work it takes to heal. In any case, the dreams will repeat for as long as you are continuing that pattern, so take note! Pay attention to what your dreams are telling you and what is going on in your life during the period you're having them.

Continuing to have the same dream can help you release your attachment to fears that have been holding you back. Your dream guide and your higher self will bring forward a worry and allow you to get used to it. If you had to deal with it in your waking life, you'd probably avoid the issue, but when your conscious mind gets pushed out of the way, you feel ready to handle it. The common dream scenarios of being late to an important event or showing up naked to school are good examples of how they help you work through insecurities. These particular narratives represent a fear of revealing too much about yourself to others or about being known on a deeper level.

Recurring dreams can also serve as warnings. For example, I (Doreen) kept having dreams about a man breaking into my bedroom and stealing my purse. I later realized that someone very close to me was embezzling money. As soon as I got the message and put a stop to the thievery, the dreams ended.

Ask your guardian angels to help you decipher recurring dreams and they will.

Eileen has been having a recurring dream for a few decades. In it, she encounters a deep, dark cave.

She wants to break through the door that stands between her and the cave, but cannot. She feels herself being sucked toward the opening as if by gravity, and as she inches closer, she becomes more fearful.

But before Eileen can reach the entrance, a legion of angels flood the darkness of the cave with light. Eileen finds she has the ability to fly and to direct energy from the palms of her hands to move objects. While she knows she can use this energy to break down the door, she never does. The angels tell her that she is all right, and that she is not meant to destroy that barrier. Eileen then realizes that she is in her childhood home. The dreams always end with her flying to heal or rescue someone. She feels she cannot do so until the angels come along—and they always do.

The cave in Eileen's dream represents her inner self. In most dreams, a home or building symbolizes your inner self or body (consider how the body "houses" your self). Eileen's afraid to see what lies within her and what work she needs to do to clear away what no longer serves her, such as repressed memories or self-deprecating feelings. Yet her higher self is trying to pull her into caring for herself, as represented by the gravity pulling her toward the cave. The door is Eileen's barrier that holds the workings of her deepest self back.

The angels help shed light on her inner workings, and once Eileen can see clearly, there is no fear. Suddenly, she realizes her power and has the confidence to transcend her barriers. She recognizes that she can heal the issues she is holding on to, but that she needs to do this in her own time. Being back in her childhood home represents feelings of safety and her desire to feel as secure as she did then.

The last part of Eileen's dream symbolizes her desire to help others, with the knowledge that she cannot do it alone. Before she can give to others, she must help herself by asking the angels for assistance. Eileen's recurring dream reminds her that the angels are always protecting her. She is shown that with their help, she can do anything. After all, the angels are extensions of Source.

Chapter Six

PAST-LIFE AND
PROPHETIC DREAMS

As we've said, in dreamtime we are not restricted
to a certain place or time. Past-life dreams and prophetic dreams are two special ways that we are able
to travel through time to learn valuable lessons for
the present.

Past-Life Dreams

The dreamtime is one way you're able to explore
lives that you had in another time period. Understanding who you once were, and how you acted
then, can shed light on a situation you're having in
the present. The purpose of past-life dreaming is to
heal emotional trauma, to regain a gift or talent that
you honed in your past life, and to heal unexplained
fears or relationships.

Past-life dreams are fun to explore. Oftentimes you'll be in a place you've never visited in your waking reality; however, it will seem as familiar as home. If you are drawn to a foreign country such as Malta, Peru, or Egypt, it is quite possible that you once had a life there. Look around in your dream and gather clues about the time period, as well as the country. You may notice that the clothes you're wearing belong to a different era, such as a Victorian dress or a medieval cloak. Similarly, if you observe any unusual buildings, customs, or anything else that is foreign to your waking life, try to remember these features so that you can research information about them later. For example, the language you speak may no longer exist, yet it will make perfect sense to you. Upon awakening, take notes in your journal and make an audio recording of any words or sentence fragments that you recall.

During a past-life dream you will look different physically, yet you'll still have some qualities similar to your present self. For example, your eyes may look the same, but your hair will be a different color and length. When you look at others, you may recognize people by their eyes, perhaps, but not any other aspect of their appearance. The person may be a family member, friend, romantic partner, teacher, or acquaintance.

When you have a past-life dream, it is often for one of the following purposes:

Relationship healing: You may have a relationship to heal from a past life, which causes this dream to be brought forward. Healing this issue usually entails that you hold the conscious intention to forgive yourself and the other person for past pain. Through forgiveness, you balance karma and break the wheel of reincarnation so that you no longer have to continue crossing paths and experiencing connections with this person. A dream may also help you remember your life mission, as well as any agreements you made with other souls before your current incarnation.

Skill recollection: You may have skills that you developed in previous lifetimes that would be useful to employ now. Perhaps you've never been confident in your abilities in a certain area. This is when a past-life dream will occur—to remind you of your true power and competency. For example, if you were a medicine woman in a previous incarnation and you now have need of your healing knowledge, you will dream of that time period. When you awake, you will remember those skills and have the confidence to use them again in this lifetime. You will also gain clarity and courage.

Soul retrieval: Imagine a glass vase being dropped, its broken pieces scattering everywhere. In a similar way, people's souls can also "fragment," usually due to a traumatic or significant event. When pieces are left in another lifetime, you can regress to that life through the dreamtime in order to retrieve that bit of your soul that got left behind. This is called *soul retrieval:* integrating a part of your soul back to the whole. This is quite an intense healing process, which can be achieved through past-life dreaming.

Past-Life Puzzles

It is important to note that the following dream is not symbolic, but literal. Ellie Topley truly traveled to this sacred place to remember who she was and the knowledge she needed to bring forward.

In Ellie's dream, there was no ceiling or walls—only sky, filled with stars. There was a tall, handsome, well-built man standing behind a desk. He seemed to Ellie to be angelic and otherworldly; although he appeared to be in his late 30s, she felt he was very wise and ancient. His eyes seemed to shift between bright and dark as he smiled. When she sat down at his desk, he began to point out constellations to her.

The angelic man was resting his left hand on an ancient book. Ellie tried to peek at the cover, but could only make out the letters *Grae* . . . When he noticed her staring, the man covered up the remaining letters. He then said warmly, "I have known and loved you, EL' Izeh." When Ellie awakened from this dream, one constellation in particular still firmly remained in her mind, and she immediately drew it in her journal.

In Ellie's dream, she traveled to an astral plane and received some pieces of the puzzle to a life that she will one day need to remember. The man was most likely not an angel, but a guardian of Ellie's whom she has known many lifetimes. Rather than giving her a lot of information at once, he seemed to be giving her a past-life message in bits and pieces so she wouldn't become overwhelmed.

The constellations may have been a reminder to Ellie of where she originated before coming to earth. The book was probably a familiar one to her, and full of useful information. The man, however, allowed her to catch only a glimpse before covering up the remaining letters. He knew she would remember the rest in Divine timing.

Sometimes, in past-life dreams, we are given messages slowly, like pieces of a puzzle, so we do not overload our minds. It takes time to absorb powerful or life-changing information, so our angels and dream guides break the message down and space it out so we can assimilate it more easily. They want us to do a bit of homework by taking time to think and researching some of what we learned.

Clearing Past-Life Blockages

Sometimes, angels ask us to stand in our power to protect ourselves. They will support us and guide us as we do, so that we understand our strength and confidence. Irene Saucier was given a heavenly message in her dream to clear problems from her past so she could continue her healing work.

In Irene's dream, she was standing on a hill in a battlefield, her long hair blowing in the wind. She was dressed in ancient armor with a solid breastplate and sandals that covered her lower legs, holding a sword in her right hand and a shield in her left. A friend stood next to her, wearing similar armor and a crimson cape. She had the impression that he was the general.

With her friend by her side, Irene began running down the hill. She felt very strong and had immense stamina as she swept her sword from left to right, clearing the path of the enemy. She did not see any actual faces of the enemy; she just sensed their presence. She struck repeatedly until there was a clear, wide path.

Then a vehicle came up the path toward Irene and her friend, which looked like a cross between a chariot and an old car. It stopped in front of them, and an angel with golden hair and a molded golden breastplate rolled down the vehicle's window. Looking at the two friends, he told them that their path was safe and they could continue on their journey. Irene recognized this angel as Archangel Gabriel as she and her friend walked down the cleared path to continue their lightwork.

Here, the clothes point to a past life in ancient Rome. It seems that Irene carried over some unresolved issues from a former lifetime. She needed to work out these problems before she could continue her journey, which was represented by clearing enemies from her path. Gabriel and her dream guide likely felt that she needed to embrace her power in order to get past this issue blocking her. They used Irene's Roman warrior lifetime to remind her of how strong and confident she had been before. So this is an example of a past-life dream for skill recollection.

In Irene's dream, she felt the "enemy" lurking about, although she could not see them. It's possible that she was harmed for doing her lightwork in another lifetime or in this Roman lifetime. This could be what Archangel Gabriel was trying to encourage her to clear, but it could also be other emotional, mental, or spiritual problems. Whatever the case may be, Irene's progress and growth were blocked. If she reviewed her present life for repeating patterns, she would discover what this unresolved issue might be. It is a condition that is likely to be present throughout many of her lifetimes.

Prophetic Dreams

Prophetic dreams show you the future and may involve personal or global situations. They often feel very real, as if you are awake, and the images you see may be symbolic or literal. They contain messages for the purpose of healing, shifting a situation, or sending prayers.

To discern whether your dream is indeed prophetic, notice if one or more of the following occurs:

- In the dream, your senses are heightened. Colors and emotions are vivid and unforgettable.

- You see things in groups of threes, such as three rings, three balloons, or three people standing in front of you.

- You see circular objects or shapes, such as a round table, people standing in a circle, or a drum.

- You awaken with the certainty, a deep intuition, that the dream will come to fruition.

In other words, you know without a doubt that it will become reality.

If you have a prophetic dream about yourself, it is either preparing you to deal with the situation or alerting you so that you have time to shift the outcome. It is important to understand the timing of a prophetic dream. It could take a day, a week, a month, a year, or even longer for what you saw to become reality—and, if you have done work on the situation, it may not *ever* become reality.

Sometimes the information you get in a prophetic dream is not meant to be shared, such as in a situation you can do nothing about. In this circumstance, the reason for the prophetic dream is so that you can send prayers to the situation or the people you dreamed of.

For example, when I (Doreen) was in college during the 1980s, I had a clear dream of people eating cheese and becoming deathly ill. The next day, I mentioned this to another student. The other girl gasped and said that she'd just heard on the news that there was a mass recall of contaminated cheese—and I hadn't yet read or heard that day's news! Because there was nothing I could do about the situation, I knew it was a dream asking me to prayerfully help. (I gave up eating cheese altogether a few years later.)

Similarly, my brother Ken clearly dreamed of the Challenger space shuttle exploding the week before it happened. Of course, he could do nothing about it. When we dream of news stories before they take place, it's clear that we're supposed to pray that everyone involved is lifted into the light.

Prophecies from Angels

Sometimes dreams are prophetic because an angel or guide is telling the dreamer the outcome of a situation. Although these dreams are rare, they do happen.

Carolina Lopez-Aregullin needed reassurance that everything was going to be all right, so she asked for a sign from Heaven. That night, she dreamed of a tornado heading toward her house. She hurried to a shelter with her husband and son, then suddenly had the feeling to look through the window. There, she saw a glowing white angel. Carolina felt that this was Divine beauty as she gazed at the angel's wings, white tunic, and long brown hair.

The angel was holding an elderly lady in a wheelchair. She had big blue eyes and white hair, and she seemed to know Carolina. Carolina felt entranced as she looked out at the lady and the angel, even though her husband kept screaming that she needed to stay away from the window. Then, just as the tornado was about to hit their home, the sun came out. The tornado was gone! Carolina's angel and the old lady were also gone.

Carolina's dream was a message to reassure her that all was well in the situation she was worried about. Her guardian angel was reminding her that she must have faith and trust her guidance, even when others around her may be afraid. The sun coming out after the storm represents a new beginning, that light will always shine after the darkness. Carolina now knows that she has support even in stressful and scary situations, as represented by the angel and elderly lady standing out in the storm. (The lady may well have been an ancestor.) Carolina is happy that even in the worst circumstances, her angels are always with her.

Connie remembers her dream of hope and peace when she was having trouble in her life.

She dreamed that there was a dark cloud in the sky that began moving in an unusual manner. As Connie watched, the cloud coalesced into a flock of black birds, which continued to fly in the same swirling patterns as the cloud. Then, one by one, the black birds began transforming into a flock of white doves, also flying in the same swirling pattern. Finally, one by one, the doves transformed into angels. The angels sang as they broke the pattern and flew in all directions across the sky.

In dreams, angels are very often symbolized by birds. Black birds denote transition or manifestation. Doves represent grace, peace, and hope. In Connie's dream, the angels were showing her that hope and peace will come to her in the situation she was concerned about.

Chapter Seven

VISITS FROM PASSED-OVER LOVED ONES

Loved ones who have passed away, including family, friends, and others you have known, can communicate to you through the dreamtime. The purpose of these dreams is to send you a message of healing, comfort, forgiveness, support, guidance, and connection. The images you see in these dreams can be symbolic, while others are meant to be taken literally. In other words, sometimes you will be shown symbols to help you understand their message, and sometimes you will simply see or hear their message directly.

When the departed appear to you in dreams, they are *truly* visiting you. Sometimes, they come to say good-bye just before they leave this earthly realm. If you encounter a passed-over loved one with whom you did not have a healthy relationship, the person is usually asking for forgiveness and wants to mend the past hurts.

In fact, Dr. Ian Stevenson of the University of Virginia conducted many studies on near-death experiences and dream visitations from the departed. His conclusions were that human consciousness survives the body's physical death and that our deceased loved ones really do visit us in our dreams!

Archangels Michael and Azrael help the departed connect with us during dreamtime. Archangel Azrael oversees the passing of loved ones and is known to help people transition from one life to the next. Guardian angels also arrive in our dreamtime to facilitate our communication with our loved ones. We will not see those angels at the time, but they are always there.

We have heard many tales of people's visits from their dearly departed. We hope that the following stories bring you comfort and hope.

Heather Hansen met and talked with a beloved friend in dreamtime who had passed over 19 years ago. Although Heather doesn't remember the exact words of the conversation they shared, she does recollect feeling anxious in a crowded environment before she found him. She also recalls the wonderful calm and serenity that followed their visit. When Heather awoke, she was invigorated by the experience.

·★·★

A few days after Summer discovered that her dad's roommate, Gordon, had passed away, she began having dreams about him. In one significant dream, she was sitting with Gordon on a patio, having a conversation. He took her inside the condo, then told Summer that he needed to leave. He gave her a hug before Archangel Michael took him up the stairs.

Gordon needed to say good-bye to Summer for healing purposes. Archangel Michael brought them together so they could hug one last time. Gordon ushering her from the outside patio to inside the condo signified his transition. Walking up the stairs with Archangel Michael represented Gordon ascending to another place—some would call it Heaven.

·★·★

Diane was praying that her nephew who'd recently passed away was surrounded by angels. That night, she had a clear dream of her nephew sitting at a celebration, surrounded by loving people who wore flowing white clothing.

Diane knows that the angels were showing her that they were with her nephew. The dream was a confirmation that her prayers had been answered.

· ★ ·

Joanne lost her brother Patrick in July of 1992. He had been 20 years old. Joanne had been like a mother to Patrick and always worried about him. A month after his passing, she woke up from what she thought was a dream. Patrick was sitting on the end of her bed smiling at her. He said, "Don't worry, Wanny. I am okay." (Wanny was Patrick's nickname for Joanne.) He reached out to hug her, then disappeared. To Joanne, the exchange in her dream felt real.

A few days later, one of Joanne's girlfriends, Pam, decided that she needed a night out to cheer her up. Even in her grief, Joanne could tell something was bothering her friend. Finally, Pam spoke up. She said that a few nights ago, she woke up from a dream to find Patrick sitting on the end of her bed. He said, "Tell Wanny that I am okay." Then he was gone.

Pam had been afraid to tell Joanne because very few people knew Patrick's nickname for her. She felt that Joanne needed to hear this message, but she didn't know until that moment that they had received the *same* message. The friends laughed and cried all the way to their destination.

Patrick knew his beloved sister needed comfort from him, and he found a way to be certain she received it—twice.

• ★ •

Sherree lost her brother, Craig, eight years ago, when he was 29. Craig had a tough time before he passed over. A year after his passing, Sherree had an incredibly vivid dream.

In the dream, Sherree was on holiday in a place that wasn't familiar to her. Since it was warm, she had left her family inside a restaurant while she went out to catch some fresh air. As Sherree walked toward the door, she noticed a stunning girl with long blonde hair sitting on the floor. Walking over to her, Sherree told her she was the most beautiful being she had ever seen.

The girl stood up and smiled at Sherree. It was then that Sherree noticed how incredibly tall she seemed. She towered above Sherree's 5'8" frame, making her at least 7 feet tall. The lovely girl said, "Sherree, I have a surprise for you."

Sherree turned to ask how she knew her name—and there stood Craig. He looked fantastic, just as he had before. He even looked years younger. Tears started flowing down Sherree's cheeks as she called for her dad, who is a nonbeliever in the afterlife. She wanted her dad to see Craig alive and well.

This dream gave Sherree great peace, as she has always had great faith in the angels and their connection to Spirit. She believes that the beautiful girl was her brother's guardian angel. We do, too.

• ★ •

Rachel and her friend, whom we'll call Tim, were extremely close throughout high school and college. Rachel felt they always had a special bond, always knowing what the other was thinking.

The month after they graduated, both friends went through big life transitions. In June of 2003, Rachel became pregnant and Tim lost his younger brother in an accident. The two best friends helped each other through all of these joyful and difficult times. Years later, Tim passed, and Rachel felt a deep loss. Then she had a dream in which she was able to say good-bye to Tim.

In Rachel's dream, it was the present day, and she and Tim were together at college. Tim kept telling Rachel that he was leaving to be with his boyfriend. Rachel could feel the ache in her heart as the time was drawing nearer for him to leave. She grabbed hold of Tim, embracing him tightly to let him know she loved him. She then looked down, and there appeared to be a little metal angel wearing a red dress, smiling up at her in the grass.

Awakening from the dream, Rachel could still feel the warmth in her heart from Tim's hug. She realized then that she needed to give that hug as much as Tim needed to receive it. Rachel also knew that the angel was a sign, to give her that confirmation that she truly had visited with her best friend.

Departed loved ones can visit more than once to help, comfort, and support us. Jeri Stith had many dream visitations from her best friend, Kathy, who had passed away ten years ago from a sudden brain aneurysm at age 44.

Kathy was a breathtakingly beautiful woman, with raven hair and eyes so deep blue that their intensity sometimes startled Jeri. However, even more startling than Kathy's beauty was her humility. She often performed kind deeds in secret, and she possessed a natural counseling ability and a lighthearted spirituality. They were each other's closest confidantes.

With an open heart, Kathy was always in awe of God and nature. She enjoyed doing things such as pointing out to Jeri the significance of certain numbers, like the address on the little 100-year-old church (111), as well as other combinations of the numbers 7 and 11 on license plates and clocks. Kathy also opened up Jeri's awareness to the spiritual significance of feathers. To Jeri, Kathy vibrated with life. One can understand the devastation Jeri felt at Kathy's sudden passing.

On a hot July night, a month after this tragic event, Jeri and her son were sleeping outside in the backyard, when she had a vivid dream about a brilliant wall of light that seemed to move like water. In the dream, Jeri was waiting by this wall for Kathy to get ready for church, and Kathy was running late. She sat patiently waiting for her, as she always had. Then Jeri saw her—Kathy was radiant! In that moment, Jeri realized that the wall of light she was seeing was the Holy Spirit. When she awakened, she was elated and knew that Kathy was absolutely fine. Jeri felt peaceful having visited with Kathy during her dream.

On another occasion, Jeri dreamed that she, her boyfriend, and Kathy were sitting together on a grandstand. Kathy pointed out that while Jeri was holding hands with her boyfriend, he was secretly using his other hand to clasp hands with another girl. Kathy was still watching out for Jeri by letting her know that her boyfriend was unfaithful!

In a third dream, Jeri saw Kathy peeking around a corner in a kitchen. She feels this was Kathy's way of watching over her. And in a fourth dream, Kathy pulled

Jeri aside into a bedroom to warn her against leaving her son alone with a potentially abusive person.

Jeri feels that Kathy is one of her guardian angels who has looked after her and her son for the past ten years. In fact, shortly after Kathy's passing, when Jeri was standing in front of a coffeehouse, she looked down to find a beautiful white feather! It was Kathy's calling card.

* ★ *

Passed-over loved ones can visit us to let us know why they left, as Ashlea discovered. In her dream, Ashlea was sitting with her grandma in the living room. With tears in her eyes, Ashlea walked into the kitchen, leaving her grandma behind. When she returned to the living room, she saw her grandma unconscious in her chair, with her spirit standing in front of the body. Her spirit appeared white, with a golden glow and subtle wings. Ashlea felt as if she were catching her grandma trying to leave again, only after she returned from Heaven.

Ashlea felt desperate as she screamed for her grandma to stay. But the elderly woman just looked at her with the same look she would always give if she thought Ashlea was asking for too much. Ashlea noticed how exhausted she looked and knew her grandma's answer was no. Turning, the spirit left.

Ashlea awakened feeling refreshed. She felt as if she really had seen her grandma—and indeed she had! Ashlea feels that her dream of her beloved grandma leaves no doubt that she is at peace in Heaven. She now knows that it was her grandma's time to go, so that she could rest.

Irene's husband passed away 32 years ago at age 29. He comes to her often in dreams. This particular dream gave Irene a rare gift she will always cherish.

In Irene's dream, she and her husband were both dressed in white, and Irene had flowers in her long hair. The feeling of tenderness between them was very strong, and they held hands as they walked down a country lane. Huge oak trees on either side of the dirt road provided deliciously cool shade. The couple felt the earth beneath their bare feet. They smelled fresh grass, moist earth, and blooming flowers.

As they walked, they encountered other couples similarly dressed and holding hands, walking down the same road. As they continued farther, the crowds became thicker. The atmosphere took on the feeling of excitement similar to approaching a concert.

Turning a corner, they saw a huge Coliseum-like building, similar to ancient Roman architecture but with a modern twist. Everyone began walking over the green pastures that led to the building. The crowds grew and couples were pushed apart. Due to the push of the crowd, Irene's beloved husband veered off toward the left. He looked over his shoulder at Irene, giving her a reassuring look.

As Irene entered the Coliseum, she turned left, where she could still see her husband walking. Unexpectedly, a beautiful angel blocked her path and said that it wasn't time for her to go in that direction. Irene noticed that the angel was golden from head to toe: long golden waves of hair, golden wings, and a long flowing gown of gold. Her feet were bare, and she carried a golden staff in one hand.

When Irene awoke, she immediately understood that she had seen a bit of Heaven. She realized she had been allowed a tender moment with her husband. In that moment, Irene knew that those who moved to the right when the couples parted were those who had to return to Earth.

Passed-Over Animals

Visits from the departed can also include our beloved pets. Oftentimes animals want to support us, reassure us, and just say hello. Your dream guide, along with Archangel Ariel and your higher self, will arrange this meeting for you and your cherished animal in dreamtime. Archangel Ariel is a protector of animals and helps them cross over.

Just as with people, when your pets visit you in dreams, they are truly there with you, saying they love you. They want you to know that they are healthy and happy; and they want you to be, too.

Geraldine lost her dear ten-year-old dog, Brazen, to a swift and aggressive illness. In a matter of four days, Geraldine had to make the heartbreaking decision to put the dog to sleep. It was the most difficult and trying time for Geraldine, as Brazen was her soul mate and greatest teacher. At the time of her death, the dog weighed 44.4 pounds. Afterward, anytime Geraldine saw the number 4, it made her think of her loss.

On New Year's Eve, although Geraldine was grieving, she and her husband went out for dinner. Checking her coat in at the restaurant, Geraldine noticed that the tag had the number 44 on it. She knew it was Brazen's way of letting her know she was celebrating with her and her husband. It didn't take long for Geraldine to realize that Brazen had become her spirit guide. The dog shows up in Geraldine's dreams to send her messages.

One evening, Geraldine dreamed that Brazen met her in a colorful landscape. Here, the dog was running freely with other beautiful creatures. The land was so vibrant and alive with love. Another evening Geraldine dreamed that Brazen showed her a place between the finite and the infinite. During her dream visitations, Geraldine feels an overwhelming sense of knowingness and understanding. Geraldine misses her dog's physical presence dearly. Yet, even in the afterlife, Brazen continues to be Geraldine's greatest teacher.

In January of 2002, after conferring with her veterinarian, Ellen made the difficult decision to euthanize her very ill ten-year-old dog. Despite Ellen's resolve that it was the right thing to do, she experienced tremendous grief afterward. She cried all day, and even in her sleep.

One night Ellen dreamed she was in Heaven, and her beloved dog was there. She asked him to verify that he was truly in Heaven by giving her a sign. Ellen asked that the sign be the wind blowing. After a moment, Ellen heard the wind blowing! She felt so happy for the confirmation that her dog was safe. Ellen awakened the next morning and felt as if someone had snapped his fingers and cleared away her grief—it was completely gone!

Ellen's husband told her that he had watched her crying in her sleep. He then noticed she began talking to someone, her eyes still closed. She took a big inhalation, followed by a long exhalation, and rolled over, before settling into restful sleep again.

A few days later, Ellen visited her grandmother, Betty, in a nursing home. Ellen expected that she would be scolded for grieving so much over a dog, particularly since three of Betty's children had died very young. Ellen told her about her strange night of sleep and sudden healing from her intense grief. Betty then shared about her own grief and healing.

In the late 1920s, Betty's two-year-old daughter died of scalding after falling into the bucket used to wash clothes. Betty grieved intensely for months. One night she dreamed of her daughter. In the dream, she saw her little girl marching in a line with a bunch of other children. Betty cried out for her daughter, who scowled as she said, "Stop it—you are holding me back." When Betty awakened, her grief was gone.

After Betty shared this dream with her granddaughter, they were certain that they both experienced otherworldly healing from grief.

Chapter Eight

Nightmares

You have a nightmare when your energy is depleted, you're extremely exhausted, or your vibration is low. When this happens, instead of walking through a portal into a higher-vibrating place during dreamtime, you walk into a low-vibrating, negative, scary place where your fears reside.

You can be influenced by such things as violent video games, movies, television, and newspaper stories, which in turn influence where you go on your night journeys. Your energy field is lowered when you are watching or participating in any kind of violent activity, and this then opens portals or gateways into the lower dream states that we call nightmares. These lower dream states hold negativity, fears, and other darker energies. You will slip through this doorway in your sleep because you have become vulnerable by allowing these negative energies to permeate your mental, emotional, and spiritual well-being.

It is important to steer clear of negative energies during your waking life. It's also imperative for you to clear your energy fields and subtle energy bodies, as well as your physical body, to stay balanced, healthy, and attuned to the higher-energy vibrations that allow you to grow, progress, and create the life you desire for the highest good of all concerned.

If you happen to find yourself slipping into a nightmare, rest assured that you are protected. Your dream guide and angels, such as Archangel Michael, will help you exit this fearful dream. Sometimes people become curious, and they might walk into the realm of a nightmare to have a look around. Of course, they quickly realize they want to leave. Again, Archangel Michael, along with their dream guide, will rescue them. Others will fall into this fearful realm when they are feeling ill, because they're mentally, emotionally, and physically vulnerable in their weakened state. Of course, their dream guide and Archangel Michael will help them out then, too.

Archangel Michael is a protector and guiding light. He often works with your dream guide when you need protection and support. He can also act as a guide during dreamtime to show you which choices would benefit your highest good. When going to bed, call upon your dream guide and any other beings of love and light to protect you during your travels.

Jennifer dreamed she was traveling and needed to make an overnight stop, when she came across a two-story white weatherboard house. Although there was no signage, Jennifer knew she could get a room for the night. She stopped the car, entered the house, and carried her bags to a large room upstairs.

When she entered her room, she was surprised to find it completely empty. An uneasy feeling came over her. She quickly turned to walk out of the room, but the door slammed shut. A key in the door turned, locking itself. Jennifer felt scared.

Suddenly, Jennifer realized she was dreaming. She knew she could change her circumstances in her dream and manifest the next events, so she immediately asked for Archangel Michael's help. She asked him to take away her fear and give her the strength to deal with this situation.

All fear immediately left Jennifer. The door unlocked itself and opened. She picked up her bags and left the room. She knew Archangel Michael stayed in the room to clear and clean it, helping the frustrated spirit that had trapped her move on.

When Jennifer awakened, she felt relief and happiness flood her. Jennifer knows she can always count on Archangel Michael's help and protection.

Amanda had a very vivid dream with Archangel Michael. Amanda and her grandmother were going downstairs into the basement with another woman. There was a confused spirit there, and Amanda felt scared. She ran up the stairs, away from the spirit.

When Amanda was outside, she invoked Archangel Michael's presence to protect everyone. He appeared with a giant shield and helped the spirit reunite with loved ones. Then he placed a protective bubble around Amanda. She realized she'd asked Archangel Michael for protection, and that's exactly what he provided. Amanda felt Divinely safeguarded. It was beautiful.

As a young child, Diana was very vocal about seeing Jesus, spirits, guides, angels, and passed-over loved ones. However, by the time she reached her preteens, she began to doubt everything, as others encouraged her to let go of her "childhood fantasies." Diana had absolutely no one in her life to talk to about these subjects, and she became very quiet and introverted about her spirituality. She began asking the angels for signs and support.

One night Diana was having a nightmare. When she awoke in the middle of the night, she didn't want to bother her parents, so she lay awake and tried to occupy herself for a couple of hours. She read books, and then rearranged her bookshelf. Nothing was calming her down. Finally, Diana decided she would try to sleep with all of the lights on. This way she could pretend she was napping in the middle of the day. She asked the angels to protect her and help her have a sound sleep.

Diana fell asleep very quickly and reentered the same terrifying dream. Suddenly, she heard beautiful music; it sounded like it was from a Disney movie. Diana realized she was dreaming, but she felt as if she were awake. She looked up at her bedroom lamp and saw four cherub angels circling the light. Diana immediately relaxed and felt at peace. She knew she was safe.

When Diana awakened in the morning, all the lights were off. Her door was closed, and the books she'd been reading were back on the shelf. Diana immediately thought of the angels she saw in her dream. However, logic took over and she was sure it was her mother.

Diana went into the kitchen, where her mother, father, and sister had gathered. She thanked her mom for coming into her room last night and turning off the lights. But Diana's mother looked puzzled and said she didn't go into her room. Diana asked her father and sister if they had gone into her room. Neither had even known she was up last night.

Diana realized that the angels had cared for her and protected her in the night. She was overjoyed. She knew she could trust that the angels are always present.

Jessica was dreaming that she was staying in the upstairs of a large Victorian house. She was with all the popular girls from school, whom she never hung out with. The house was very large, but not quite big enough to be a mansion.

Suddenly, it began to storm outside. Trees were thrashing about in the harsh winds, and lightning flashed and thunder clapped as large raindrops poured down from the skies. There was an impending sense of danger, intense negativity, and absolute mayhem. A tall dark figure ran about the room, throwing things around and setting items on fire. The girls were huddled together in a corner, scared, as the entity grew larger and more powerful.

Jessica began praying, which was unusual for her. Suddenly, Archangels Raphael and Michael appeared in the middle of the room. They began fighting off this negative entity. Jessica could see Michael's fiery sword and Raphael's green aura surrounding all of the girls. Raphael looked at Jessica with his gorgeous green eyes and told her everything had been taken care of and that they were safe.

Jessica awakened immediately after, grasping for her rosary. She was amazed by how safe and protected she felt.

Our angels and dream guide can teach us how to help ourselves in dreamtime. A woman named Destiny discovered from her angels this method to get out of any scary dream:

Whenever Destiny finds herself in a nightmare, she becomes lucid in her dream. As described in Chapter 3, lucid dreaming means being aware that you are asleep; in other words, you realize during the dream that you are dreaming. So at any time, Destiny can close her eyes in a bad dream and think of a place that is safe. Once she opens her eyes, she will be in that safe place.

This is a great method that anyone can learn to do. Thanks, Destiny!

Chapter Nine

FLYING AND FALLING DREAMS

Soaring through the sky in dreamtime can be both exhilarating and freeing. Many people have dreams about flying, teaching others to fly, and learning how to fly, and they report that it always feels vivid and real. Dreamers often remember a specific technique they employ when flying. We will discuss these methods in this chapter.

Flying dreams often indicate a need for the freedom to express yourself. These types of dreams can also be guidance for you to take a "leap of faith" and move forward fearlessly. Symbolically, they mean that if you take a risk in life, you will not fail/fall, but "fly."

Angels will help people fly during dreamtime to show them a message through a bird's-eye view. They may also be trying to remind people that they, too, have physical abilities of flight. Angels want to tell us that we can all metaphorically fly: just believe in yourself and your connection to Source. By passing this message along, the angels remind us of our inherent power to overcome the limitations of waking reality— of life, in other words. We are, in fact, limitless.

Techniques of Flying

The very first rule of flying is that you must believe you can!

There are several techniques to flying in dreams. All are equally effective.

Spreading Your Arms to Glide

The first flying method is to glide or soar with your arms open wide. Your arms act like wings that support you on the air thermals.

Zoe frequently dreams of flying without wings attached to her; she simply spreads her arms. She feels an ease and weightlessness when she soars, flying vertically and horizontally, like Superman. During some dreams, she sees herself floating inside buildings. In many, however, Zoe has a fear of soaring higher. She senses she can reach further but is afraid of doing so. Flying can symbolize freedom, self-expression, and growth, so the fear of going higher may signal that Zoe is afraid of self-growth.

Flying with Wings

The second flying method involves having wings like a bird or an angel.

Tereze has had many types of dreams, and she often employs different flying techniques (for example, in one dream she used her mind to hover over the ground). In the most memorable flying dream, Tereze discovered she was an eagle! As this exceptional creature, she could feel the wind in her brown feathers. She knew how to orient herself in the air by utilizing the air currents.

In eagle form, Tereze felt so carefree and unbound by limitations. Dreaming of eagles symbolizes homing in on detail in your life, and looking at life with a new perspective. It also represents spiritual visions and healing.

Flapping Your Arms

The third method for flying in dreams involves flapping your arms like a bird flaps its wings.

One of Courtney's flying techniques is spreading her arms to glide and "swimming." During some dreams, flapping her arms to fly feels like she's performing the breaststroke through the air.

One night, Courtney had a dream in which she was riding a horse. She had a long journey ahead, so

Courtney began flying in order to arrive at the destination more quickly. Horses represent movement, new journeys, and stretching your freedom and power. Perhaps this last dream is a reflection of Courtney's urgency to move forward in her personal power.

Using Mental Power to Fly

The fourth method for dream flying involves your mind alone. In these dreams, you make the decision to fly . . . and it happens! For some people, the flying is an unconscious act without any mental strain. For others, there's a steady sense of controlling the movement through the power of the mind.

Courtney, the woman in the last story, uses another technique to fly, this one involving "thinking" herself into the air. Sometimes she levitates, while other times she is flying high in the sky, over large bodies of water, or in the clouds.

Another woman, Claudia, has experienced flying dreams since she was a little child, and her technique also usually consists of pure belief. She teaches others how to fly in dreams, too. She explains that it's all mind control and breathing. You must be relaxed and breathe deeply, and only then will you begin to levitate.

In one recent dream, Claudia flew high in the sky, as if pulled by a force from above. She levitated, as if her body were lighter than air. In another dream, Claudia flew above a skyscraper over the city of Leipzig, Germany. She was enjoying a wonderful view, as if she were on a plane, completely weightless, free, and happy.

Similarly, Michelle has always had flying dreams. She usually dreams she is traveling over towns and cities, watching everyone going about their business. Occasionally, she will stop to help or talk to someone. She has complete control over her flying. Although she can move herself up and down, backward and forward, with her arms, Michelle mainly uses her mind to guide her body where she wants to be. She uses her arms for balance and her thoughts to fly. She need only have the thought to be somewhere and instantly she flies there.

Although Michelle has had, and continues to have, many flying dreams, she always feels as if she's flying for the first time. When she becomes aware in her dream that she is flying, she is surprised and ecstatic. She flies with such ease and grace, as though it is a normal part of everyday life. She feels great strength, confidence, and freedom, like nothing else matters. These dreams make her realize that she has always had this same strength and knowledge within herself.

Upon waking from her flying dreams, Michelle always feels as if something has been released. It seems to her that the energy she accumulated during the day within her body has been discharged. Michelle is then left with a sense of calmness and peace.

As you can see, flying dreams also help to release unwanted energies, remove boundaries, and build confidence.

Running into Flight

The fifth method for flying in dreams involves running fast, like an airplane gaining speed on a runway before takeoff. Some people jump at the end of their run, and others simply take off.

Stina has recurring dreams of flying. She begins running, then suddenly she lifts off the ground. Stina moves her hands so she can navigate. Her dreams usually consist of flying above the area where she used to live. She is alone, looking down on the buildings and everything underneath her. Sometimes she flies over a soccer field, a playground, and open fields. Other times, there are people on the ground looking up at her, amazed that she knows how to fly.

Sometimes Stina cannot stay flying in the air. When this happens, she may need to land abruptly, but her landing is always safe. Stina constantly feels as if she is in full control and experiences an exhilarating sense of freedom and grace.

Leaning into Flight

The sixth method for flying in dreams is to stand up, lean forward, and let the air thermals carry you into the sky.

Angie's flying technique is to stand, angle her body, and lift up into the air. She floats and moves ahead with intent. While it's happening, she feels as if her flying ability is mind-driven. She simply makes the decision to become lighter, and her body cooperates and begins to fly. However, Angie feels like flying is fragile. She worries that if fear is allowed in, her ability would disappear.

Again, the belief, trust, and confidence in your ability to fly is necessary. Flying dreams teach us to believe—in ourselves, our abilities, and the innate gifts we have been given.

Out-of-Body Experiences

Oftentimes, people have *out-of-body experiences,* or OBEs. A common time for them is during a dream. (One type of OBE is astral traveling, which we will discuss later in the chapter.)

An OBE occurs when the dream body is off exploring. The dream body, you'll remember, melds with the physical body in much the same manner as an aura. It acts as an energetic vehicle, so you can leave your physical body sleeping while you fly to other places and times with your dream body. You can explore all of the realms as if you were experiencing them with your physical body.

Christine had an out-of-body experience where she was dreaming about standing outside her childhood home. Suddenly she began to gently lift off the ground. At first she was frightened, but then she realized an angel was actually lifting her dream body from behind. Together they soared in a lazy loop around the house and yard. Christine watched the people below.

Unexpectedly, Christine and the angel took off at an unbelievably fast speed. In a matter of seconds, they flew into outer space. Stopping for a moment, Christine looked around at the stars and planets. Zooming off again, the angel took Christine through a forest. They whizzed through the trees without ever touching a single branch. Christine thought they were looking at the earth, but suddenly they flew over a creature she described as a bear with several arms and the skin of an elephant.

Before Christine knew it, she had returned home. Her guardian angel gently set her down on the floor.

Christine remarked how much she enjoyed the adventure, and the angel replied that Christine could go wherever she desired.

A Dog's Validation of a Flying Experience

Dogs, cats, and small children can see energy clearly. Because they aren't oversocialized like human adults, animals and children are open to any experience. This allows them to clearly experience angels and other beings in the spirit world.

Shantell experienced her first flying dream when she was five years old. She flew up from her bed, out the window of her bedroom, and over her backyard. Shantell's dog, Kinger, was in the yard and he barked and whined as he watched her fly around. Shantell thought it odd that he could see her flying since she didn't make a sound.

Shantell flew toward the clouds. When she reached them, she sat and looked around her. She felt that being in the clouds must be like being in Heaven. Then she heard a voice reply to her thought: "Yes, it is very similar." Shantell turned in the direction of the voice and asked if it was an angel. The reply was a soft yes.

Shantell then asked the angel if God was real. The angel affirmed that God was. She then inquired what it would be like *without* God. The angel asked

Shantell to put her head in the clouds. Shantell did so, and saw, felt, heard, and was aware of nothing. There was a vast emptiness. Shantell didn't like the feeling. She pulled her head out of the clouds and reported to the angel that without God, there would be nothing—she wouldn't exist, nothing would. The angel agreed.

Shantell thanked the angel and flew back to her house. Kinger began to bark again. He then walked over to Shantell's bedroom window and whined. Shantell decided to go back through the window so she could return to her physical body.

When she awakened, she told her mom about her dream. Her mom said that Kinger had been whining and barking all night, and he had clawed the house near Shantell's window. Then her mom noted that the dog was not barking anymore, nor was he acting odd. Shantell ran outside to hug Kinger. She knew he had seen her dream body flying.

Astral Traveling

Astral traveling is a special type of out-of-body experience. In some astral-travel dreams people fly, while in others they do not. The dreamer will often ascend to a mountain peak or another high point. Your dream body, which is also known as the astral body, will appear to be floating above your physical body while you sleep. Astral-traveling dreams come when you are in a liminal state, deeply relaxed.

Many ancient and modern cultures consider astral traveling to be a form of sacred dreaming used for initiation, training, and healing purposes. These dreams usually occur when there is information of worldwide importance to be shared or when the dreamer's life path needs to be powerfully impacted.

There are several ways to recognize when you are astral traveling. In your dream, you will feel a state of bliss and exultation. You may hear the music of the spheres (the sounds of the Universe and celestial bodies). Colors are supersaturated and of a hue that you will not find on this Earth plane.

The vital force of your dream (astral) body is facilitated by its exposure to cosmic energy at night. Therefore, during these higher states, you will likely encounter the cosmic assemblage also known as the High Council. This is an enlightened group of beings operating from a state of Divine love and light, who guide people toward the highest good of all. The main distinction between an out-of-body experience and astral travel is the High Council imparting information.

Usually, upon awakening from astral travel, you will have a greater sense of purpose in your life. However, you may also feel exhausted, because you may be traveling far as you offer healing to the world. In either case, know that you have received important information and performed important work.

Meeting a Member of the High Council

Sophie had been searching her heart in order to discover her life purpose. She had attended several life-changing classes, and it seemed she was on the right track. Yet she still was not sure what step to take next. She had an action plan and didn't like waiting around for something to just happen, but she spent a few weeks mulling over her career and relationships.

During this time, Sophie read several books about past lives, future lives, and manifestation. Nothing seemed to have anything new to offer. Then Sophie picked up a spiritual adventure novel that turned out to be the inspiration she needed. The book allowed her mind to relax and open up to new possibilities. Although this book was stimulating for Sophie, she still felt as if her life was slowly moving forward, with no sense of accomplishment.

A few nights later, as Sophie began to fall asleep, she heard her name being called. Her eyes flew open and she searched her room. Her heart was beating rapidly, and her forehead was damp with sweat. She realized that the voice sounded a bit mechanical, not truly human, almost like it was adjusting to the dense atmosphere. Sophie smiled as she recognized that someone, somewhere else—perhaps on another plane—was trying to get her attention. She offered a brief thank-you, relaxed, and fell asleep.

In her dream, Sophie found herself in a beautifully exotic locale. She was wearing a tan robe with waist ties, and her long hair was blowing around her shoulders. She was standing in the middle of a stone staircase on the side of a mountain. She heard a voice calling to her on the wind, asking her to keep climbing until she was at the peak of the mountain.

As Sophie climbed, she noticed that the trees, the flowers, and even the air were vibrant with colors she had not seen before on Earth. She felt a strong magnetism pulling her toward the top of the mountain. Again, the kind voice beckoned her to keep climbing. The wind was stronger near the top. Finally reaching the peak, Sophie could see the amazing world below. She felt as if past, present, and future moments were shifting visibly in the air before her.

Although she could not see the being with her, Sophie knew he was there. He appeared to meld into the air in front of her. This being seemed to be guiding Sophie to notice certain images such as a condor, a *Chakana* (a 12-point Incan cross), and a future moment she needed to recall at a later date.

Sophie also had the distinct feeling that this male being was sharing a clairsentient message with her, as if he was downloading into her some steps of her life purpose. Sophie felt safe, protected, and very loved during this process. She knew she would wake up not remembering all of the information passed on to her, but that her energetic and physical bodies would safeguard it and use it at the most appropriate time for the highest good of all concerned.

Upon awakening from this dream, Sophie felt inspired and completely alive. She no longer felt as if her life were standing still. She knew everything would open in perfect Divine timing and that she had the information necessary to employ at need. Sophie knew without a doubt that she had visited another place in time, somewhere on the astral plane where this being of Divine love and light could give her higher knowledge to be used for good. She was refreshed and ready to begin the next journey of her life purpose—and she didn't mind waiting.

Sophie's dream was indeed an astral-traveling one. Many of its qualities unmistakably indicate this: meeting a High Council member, traveling to a mountain peak or other high point, vibrant or super-saturated colors not of this world, and feeling that information was being downloaded.

The condor is a sacred spirit bird in the Incan belief system, and here it represents Sophie's clairvoy-ant abilities, as well as her sharp focus to home in on detail, her potential to soar to new heights, and visits from ancient ancestors and spirits.

The Chakana is another symbol sacred to the ancient Inca. After dreaming of this symbol, Sophie began studying its many layers of meaning. She has now begun to understand the message the member of the High Council was trying to convey to her.

Flying with the Angels

Flying with the angels denotes an open, willing heart. If you find yourself flying with them, know you are being called to possibly help the angels help someone else. The angels bring messages to assist not only us us personally, but others as well. They may use flying to help relay that message or remind you of your own powers.

The morning of December 11, 1992, Marla was dreaming that she was flying with the Celtic goddess Brigid and her angels. They took her flying over the ocean near San Diego. Marla had not been to California before, so this was an especially fun experience. They landed at a water park that Marla heard them call "Sing Me Oaks Water Park." The energy was very peaceful, and they stopped to float in a pool. It was sunny and warm; the aquamarine water was clear and beautiful, like sparkling diamonds. Brigid and the angels told Marla that they liked this water park and they always wanted it to be available, but it needed to be bigger.

When Marla awakened from this dream, all she could think about was this beautiful water park. She decided to see if it existed, so she dialed Information and asked for a place named "Sing Me Oaks Water Park near San Diego." The operator said there was a place called *Sengme* Oaks Water Park and gave Marla the phone number.

Marla felt she was called upon to relay this message from Brigid and the angels. When a woman at Sengme Oaks answered the phone, Marla shared that she had a dream about angels saying the water park needed to be available but expanded. The woman thanked Marla and said that the owner would be happy to know that. She said that he was looking for a sign because he had a board meeting in a few days that dealt with the future of the park!

Marla had another flying dream one winter. As she flew over her village with the angels, they spotted someone who had fallen in the snow who needed their help. Marla's angels told her to stop flying and wake up—she needed to come to the aid of the fallen person! Marla felt the tugging of an unseen force pulling her out of bed. She heard her angels say, "Let's go now! Quick!"

When Marla awoke, it was 5 A.M. and still dark. On top of that, there was a snowstorm outside. Marla got dressed as fast as she could, putting her coat on over her pajamas. Suddenly, she heard a jingle followed by a crash. She looked up from putting on her boots and saw that her car keys had fallen off the hook from the key rack on the door. She took the hint and quickly got in her car.

As Marla drove to the place she remembered in her dream, the car seemed to stop of its own accord. Then, in a snowbank on the side of the street, Marla saw a young man who looked to be in his late teens. She jumped out of the car and rushed over to where he was lying, covered in snow. When Marla tried to move him, he did not respond. Then she noticed a huge snowplow coming down the street, sounding its horn for her to move.

Marla prayed for God and the angels to help her lift the young man and get him quickly into her car before the snowplow arrived. When she tried to pick up the boy, he felt light as a feather. She knew that the angels were helping her, as the boy was much larger than she was, yet she was easily able to move him. As soon as she placed him inside the car, the snowplow rushed by the spot they were in, and she shouted a thanks to Heaven.

As Marla drove, the boy slowly became conscious of his surroundings. He told her that he remembered her walking past his house the other day. Indeed, Marla had walked down Pine Street the day before, so she turned in that direction. When they arrived on that street, Marla saw a woman coming out of a house, and the boy indicated that he lived there. The woman walked over to Marla and said she was the boy's mom. She had been worried because her son had gone to the 24-hour convenience store in the snowstorm to get milk for them and he had been gone over an hour. She had been preparing to go look for him.

The young man told his mother how he had fallen, hit his head, and was knocked unconscious. She thanked Marla for finding her son and helping him, and to their amazement, Marla shared the flying dream she'd had about the boy, and how the angels had helped them all.

Several years ago, Patricia had the most vivid dream of her life. The dream occurred the evening she had become lost driving in a dense fog. She'd felt uneasy and frightened, so she prayed for the angels to surround her car with protection and show her the way home. Of course, Patricia did find her way home.

That same night Patricia dreamed she was flying over the mountains with angels by her side protecting her. Patricia's mission was to land at the campfires scattered throughout the mountains and deliver information and a message of encouragement to the people at each one. Patricia felt safe, but there seemed to be a sense of urgency that she deliver her words and quickly move on to the next campfire.

As Patricia flew over the treetops, she would look down and see thousands of little glimmering lights from each camp. She knew that when the messages were all delivered, her destination was atop a mountain, on a large flat rock that formed a platform for landing. Patricia finished her mission there with a sense of accomplishment.

Patricia's dream held two messages. One message was showing her that she had information that would help others. Perhaps she needed to be of service in her community, as she had the necessary tools to help. Her dream might also be telling her that this was her mission in life, to help others. The second message was, of course, to remind Patricia of her ability to fly—that is, to take a leap of faith.

Flying Dreams Are Empowering

Flying dreams can be healing, because they allow you to rise above your physical, emotional, and spiritual problems and see the bigger picture. In this way, you can detach so that healing can occur.

For example, Brenda was extremely unhappy living in a household of alcoholics. She had her first flying dream when she was a teenager. She dreamed she was flying above her family. As they watched from below, they began pointing upward at her. She glided above, circling them in absolute freedom. Whenever Brenda has a flying dream, she feels weightless and liberated.

This dream symbolizes Brenda's ability to rise above the circumstances of her family. Her dream was showing her that she doesn't need to be afraid. She is free to make her own choices and doesn't need to carry the stress or pain of her home life around. She is able to free herself from these heavy situations. Brenda does believe her flying dreams to be a deeper, transformative connection to her soul.

Brenda is another dreamer who teaches people how to fly. In her dreams, she tells others to open their arms and give their hearts to the wind. As Brenda teaches this, the wind gently lifts her upward and soon she is flying. She usually glides smoothly, without flapping her arms.

Amanda discovered that when she flies in dreamtime, she feels completely natural and without restrictions. During most of her flying dreams, Amanda moves through the air, yet in others she will be navigating her way through trees or city buildings. Amanda noted that her dreams in city buildings do not feel nearly as uplifting as those in the trees, because the buildings are difficult to navigate.

Amanda also noticed that sometimes she flaps her arms to fly, and sometimes they are spread outward as she glides. She uses her arms to move in different directions, and she enjoys steering. She says it feels empowering to her to take charge and change direction whenever she chooses. Amanda also employs the "thinking" flying technique in her dreams. She simply points her index finger to where she wants to travel, and her body moves in that direction.

Amanda believes that her flying dreams are also past-life dreams from ancient times when we could all fly. There is a very strong possibility that this is true.

Felise had many flying dreams as a child. She recalled it being the most amazing feeling of lightness, weightlessness, and above all, joy. Felise remembered a dream in which she saw an aerial view of where she lived. In this dream she was able to move freely through dense objects. However, upon awakening, Felise felt thrust back into her body, and the feeling of denseness and limitation would return. Along with the weightless sensation, the feeling of oneness and unconditional love disappeared.

As Felise has become older, she doesn't fly anymore in dreamtime. One reason might be that she doesn't feel the same freedom of self-expression. She may feel stuck, as if she can no longer soar to new heights in her life.

Falling Dreams

Falling in a dream can signal that the dreamer feels out of control, as if he or she has unstable footing. It can also symbolize not standing in one's personal power. Perhaps the dreamer has stopped expressing his or her truth or creativity.

Some people start to fall asleep, to be suddenly awakened with a jolt because they are falling. This represents the dreamers "falling" into a portal or opening of a dream space they do not need to be entering, such as a nightmare. Therefore, their higher selves and dream guide immediately send them the falling sensation so that they wake up and begin again.

A "kick" or "fall" is a physical sensation that your subconscious gives your body to stop you from entering a dream state you know would not be beneficial for you. Then, when you fall back asleep, it's like changing the channel on the radio or television. You will have chosen another path to take in your dreams that night. Your dream guide and angels will physically touch you to get you back into your physical body, so you can start over in dreamtime.

Traelynn would periodically have dreams where she was falling. She would wake up with a sudden start, panting and scared. One night she had the same falling dream, yet this time when she was close to the ground, Traelynn suddenly spread her arms and began to fly! She flew all over the world seeing the beauty of the earth. Then, she began to see the devastation caused by humans toward the environment and wildlife.

Traelynn felt that the dream was positive because it gave her a deep passion to get involved in conservation and preservation. It also left her with the gift of fearless flying; no longer was she afraid of falling.

The angels were showing Traelynn she had the power to take control of her life and make choices for her highest good.

Chapter Ten

ANGEL MESSAGES

Dream messages can be life-changing or life-affirming. A simple hello or smile from our angels can help us awaken feeling refreshed and ready to begin our journey that day.

Some messages we receive can be meant for others or as a confirmation for ourselves. This type of dream is very straightforward, yet profound for the dreamer. An angel will arrive simply to let the dreamer know they are with them.

Archangel Michael Reassures Us of His Protection

Archangel Michael wants us to know that he is always there protecting us, as Jean Zurich discovered. And if we don't hear his message the first time, he'll make sure we get it!

Jean had been worrying about an issue all day. Then, that night, she dreamed about Archangel Michael. He was glowing with a deep golden and white light, and he held her in his arms, saying, "I have you." He sheltered her under his body while his wings protected her. At this point in her dream, Jean awakened and left her bed to get a drink of water. When she returned, she promptly fell asleep . . . and began having the exact same dream again! When Jean awakened, she realized that Archangel Michael really was there for her, protecting her. And just in case she did not believe his message the first time, he made sure that she experienced it all over again.

These two dreams continue to bring Jean much comfort when she reflects on them. Both times she awakened feeling very loved and protected. The message she received was to trust the Universe and the angels; she was safe, and they would help her resolve any situation that was bothering her.

Sometimes when we worry too much, we forget to release our concerns to the Universe. When this happens, it's not uncommon to receive a dream to remind us that the angels will take care of us.

Renée received comfort from Archangel Michael when she was worried about her daughter. He came to her in her dream to tell her that he was her daughter's guardian angel and that he would always watch over her. He said that if she, or anyone, ever needed help, all she must do to call the angels is whisper their names. Renée immediately felt a burden lift from her shoulders and relief flood her heart.

Some people are troubled by the idea that they do not belong here on the Earth plane. They might also have a fear of dying and think about this often. Our dreams are one way that our angels and guides can reassure us in the face of our worries about this kind of situation.

Although Nancy's angel dream occurred years ago when she was in high school, she remembers it as if it were yesterday. She dreamed of walking into a church, searching around for somewhere to sit. When she spotted her family, she walked over and sat down beside her brother. Everyone began singing; then, unexpectedly, Nancy began floating! She could hear a crow in the distance as she continued drifting upward, away from the church.

Then a beautiful white light appeared and surrounded Nancy. She felt a peaceful, loving warmth, which made her want to delve deeper into its comfort. The closer she moved toward the bright white light, the louder the crow cawed. Suddenly, a commanding, powerful voice boomed, "Stop! Turn around. You are not ready to come up here yet. It is not your time." Although Nancy wanted to stay in that blissful sanctuary, she turned around and floated back. The sound of the crow grew fainter and fainter, until it stopped completely.

Nancy woke up with the awareness that it was Archangel Michael who had spoken to her with that commanding yet loving voice. Floating away in her dream represented her desire to be closer to Source. The sound of the crow was a warning that she wanted to be *too* close to the light—the same light that appears when a person transitions to the Other Side. Archangel Michael, however, made it clear to her that it was not yet her time to leave her physical body; she still had more work to do on Earth. Nancy feels reassured that loving angels are always protecting and watching over her, whether in dreamtime or waking reality.

Cristina received support from an angel in a simpler dream. Cristina's dream occurred more than 50 years ago, when she was 5 years old, but she remembers it clearly.

She had always been interested in the saints and the angels. Even as a young child, she used to collect those small saint prayer cards. She would line them up and talk to them.

One night, Cristina was sleeping in bed when she turned on her right side. She saw a beautiful being standing next to her, completely surrounded by a royal-blue light. Cristina watched the being lie down next to her.

This dream had a very significant effect on Cristina at such a tender age. The being was most likely her guardian angel, letting her know that she would always be by her side. The royal-blue light also indicates that it could be Archangel Michael who visited her, undoubtedly to let Cristina know she was safe and protected.

Cristina's guardian angel made sure she would always remember this by visiting her at an impressionable age.

Angels Are Always at Your Side

You are never alone. Angels are always there with you, to support you, if you ask them. Amy Clark realized that her angel just wanted to let *her* know that she was not alone.

Amy's first angel dream happened after reading a book about angels. Before bed, she said a mental prayer asking that they visit her in her dreams. That night, Amy dreamed she saw a male angel with gray wings. Although Amy did not recall any words being exchanged between them, she sensed that he was allowing her to take a feather from his wings. Amy only briefly noticed that there might have been other heavenly beings around. However, by that point she was beginning to awaken from her dream.

As Amy fully awakened, she had an overwhelming feeling of being in a state of constant love. She felt as if she were in love with everyone. This dream proved to her that everything she had read about the feelings elicited by an encounter with an angel was true. Amy herself certainly felt intoxicated by love!

· ★ ·

It is heartwarming and inspiring to awaken from a dream where our angels are giving us proof they are truly around us.

Jacob had always asked his angels to give him a sign in his dreams. However, he never seemed to find one that he could definitively say was from an angel. Jacob was staying at his partner's house when he finally received an unmistakable sign.

In his dream, Jacob was in the living room having a conversation with his partner's parents. The conversation had nothing to do with spirituality.

Suddenly, Jacob became very aware of his partner's mother. As he began to focus on her, she turned to him and said, "Jacob . . . angels." The word *angels* was so focused and sharp that it awakened him from his dream. Jacob knew that it was a sign from his angels telling him that they were with him.

For Jacob it was such a profound dream that he awoke with a massive smile on his face.

· ★ ·

In her sweet dream message, Mary Theresa received reassurance that our angels are always listening and paying attention.

As Mary Theresa was giving thanks to her beautiful guardian angel for always being there for her, she asked if she could be given her guardian angel's name in a dream. She knew in her heart that she would be answered. The next morning, as she was awakening but still in a semi-sleep state, Mary Theresa heard distinctly, "My name is Rose."

Mary Theresa awakened completely and dissected the experience immediately before she forgot any details. Rose's voice seemed distant, like an echo from another dimension. Without any doubt, Mary Theresa knew her prayer had been answered and that her angel's name was Rose.

· ★ ·

The first time Kyna Towns dreamed of an angel, she also received a message of love. Kyna dreamed that Archangel Metatron came to see her. He was beautiful, with golden skin, long blond hair, and the most amazing blue eyes that seemed almost purple.

She remarked on his appearance. He told her that this was just how she had chosen to see him in this visit. Metatron had a message for Kyna: she needed to be nicer, he told her. Then he hugged Kyna. The hug was so powerful she never wanted it to end.

Upon awakening, Kyna thought the angel meant that she needed to be kinder to her family, friends, and those she met. However, after some time passed, Kyna began to realize that Metatron's message meant for her to be nicer to herself. She needed self-love.

· ★ ·

Karen needed an affirmation that she had been successful in her mission. One night, she dreamed she was standing before an older-looking male figure donning a colorful robe.

He shared a message with Karen that she had been successful in her mission. Karen then felt a powerful winged embrace from behind her as she and the angel began floating upward together, cheering in celebration.

· ★ ·

In the summer of 2010, Johannes said the following prayer before bed:

"Dear God, please give me a dream with clear messages about my origin, which I remember when I wake up."

That night, Johannes received a dream to confirm that there is life after life. In his dream, Johannes was lying down in a church. He knew with exact timing when he would die. He had been waiting, but now the time was here.

Johannes asked to be carried out of the room, so he could say good-bye to his family. His family gathered around him, but it was not his present-day, waking-life one. Yet he knew that this was his family from another time. He hugged each member, one by one.

Johannes then told his family to remember that there are messengers that can help them. He encouraged them to believe in them and pray. He explained that these messengers will come to them and support them in their time of need. Johannes said good-bye to everyone and hugged them one last time.

As Johannes left his earthly body, he rose up quickly. He looked down on a green earth, and an infinity sign appeared before him. Then the earth disappeared quickly as a feeling of peacefulness washed over Johannes.

Upon awakening, Johannes pondered life after life. He did not know anything about previous lives, angels, or guides. Now, however, Johannes is convinced that we are surrounded by loving angels and helpers that can aid us in our lives. He feels we must believe and pray.

A Message for <u>You</u>

Once in a while there's a dream message that is meant for all to hear. We'd like to conclude this book with Rowan Moon's dream message about Divine connection. In Rowan's story of meeting one of her angels for the first time, she received a powerful burst of faith and information. The potency of this dream is evident. The angels are amazing beings of love and light, spreading messages from God, and Rowan's encounter with her guardian angel left her with a powerhouse of a message! You will see how this message relates to you as well. Rowan was given this information to share with those who are interested. If you are reading this, that includes *you*.

· ★ ·

In the early 1990s, after Rowan realized that she had a knack for hearing messages from deceased relatives, she began to try to hear her angelic friends, too. She had always known she could talk to people whom no one else could hear or see, but she understood very little about this ability. She was on a spiritual path of discovery in her early 20s, hoping to hone this skill. She was reading many spiritual books at the time, and her sister gifted her an angel book that would change Rowan's life. In one chapter of this book, there was an exercise on how to communicate with your angels during sleep. Using this method, Rowan had a dream so vivid that she felt as if she had crossed dimensions.

In her dream, Rowan became aware that she was standing in a beautiful meadow, with a ring of trees in the distance circling around her. The grass, flowers, and faraway trees were so vibrant that it was like looking at a painting! The grass was growing wild and almost reached Rowan's knees. She waked barefoot upon the warm earth, and it was akin to walking on a heated floor. A bright yellow sun shone through fluffy white clouds.

Rowan felt an inner peace and contentment as she lazily walked through the meadow. Arriving in an area where the grass was freshly mown, she had an urge to lie down. As she stretched out, a bunny rabbit appeared at her feet. The bunny was larger than normal, and its fur was a very deep purple that seemed to shine like diamonds. Rowan was mesmerized. As she moved to touch it, it hopped away. Instinctively, Rowan followed.

As the rabbit disappeared behind a huge, ancient oak, an intense flash in Rowan's peripheral vision caught her attention. Turning, she saw a massive pillar of white light, as large as a tower, emitting a pulsating warmth that flowed over her. She walked toward it, seeing it slowly shrink to about 10 feet tall. Then suddenly, a luminescent 8-foot-tall figure with wings spanning 16 feet emerged from the light. His wings were not feathery or birdlike, but formed from silvery white filaments. The being's skin was translucent and, like the rabbit, shone with little points of lights, as if diamonds were under his skin. Rowan knew that standing before her was her guardian angel.

The angel spoke to Rowan by projecting thoughts into her mind. He shared that what she saw was not the way he truly looked, but he had shown himself in this manner because it was the only way her brain could have interpreted the experience. This angel was not a spirit that would ever live in a human body, but a guardian who would always remain in his own realm. He could move freely between dimensions, and time did not exist for him.

He told her that everyone's spirits were formed simultaneously with the Universe, and that Rowan had always been here and would always be here, though she might take on many different guises. He said that she was linked to not only him, but every other spirit on Earth and beyond. Indeed, since everyone was formed at exactly the same time, all were eternally linked to one another. The angel was guardian not only to Rowan, but to countless others, and he could fulfill his role this way because he was part of the Divine Source.

The angel explained that "every being has one life." Rowan later realized that this meant that as souls we cannot die; all will exist—and have already existed—for eternity, even if a particular human experience happens only once.

Rowan then asked her guardian angel if he had a name. He explained that those like him are all without form and do not have a gender as such. He told her that she could name him, if she found it useful for her connection with him. However, he reminded her that since her spirit is connected to his, he is always with her. He cannot leave Rowan since they are joined for eternity.

Rowan understood the significance of her guardian angel's words. She didn't need to "call" on him and ask him to join her, for he was already there. Rowan felt a love emanate from him that was overwhelming, yet powerfully calming.

The beautiful angel embraced her without touching her physically. Although he was standing opposite her, Rowan felt like someone had wrapped a warm blanket around her. She felt incredibly safe.

She closed her eyes for a moment. When she opened them, he was gone.

Rowan awoke with the realization that she had been crying as she dreamed. Her pillow and cheeks were dampened from tears. Yet Rowan felt like she was the happiest girl alive. This encounter was one of the most wonderful things she'd ever experienced.

Although Rowan prayed for this dream to occur again, it has not. She has come to realize that her angel does not need to appear as before. He is there with her even if she cannot hear him like she did in her dream.

Rowan feels an inner calmness now when she thinks about the fact that no one is ever truly alone. Rowan experiences a sense of awe at the realization that God is more powerful than the angels, and the angels have infinite cosmic power. Therefore, God is mighty, awesome, and truly omnipotent!

AFTERWORD

Dreams are gateways to creating your world and the life you want to live. They are tools for experiencing your inner self, manifesting your desires, and healing all areas of your life. Dreaming is fun, and learning to decode your dream messages is simple—everyone can do it! All it takes is a little practice and an open heart. Receiving Divine guidance through your dreams is a gift given to you by Source/God.

You are an amazing co-creator. You are a child of Divine love and light. You can create and be anything you desire.

Enjoy playing and creating in your dreamtime.
Enjoy discovering the meaning of your dreams.
Enjoy the magical journey of dreamtime!

ABOUT THE AUTHORS

 **Doreen Virtue** is a life-long clairvoyant and fourth-generation metaphysician who holds three university degrees in counseling psychology. She's the author of many books, audio programmes, and card decks about angels, psychic development and mind-body-spirit topics, including the *Angel Dreams Oracle Cards* (co-authored with Melissa Virtue).

Doreen has appeared on *Oprah*, CNN and other television and radio programmes, and writes regular columns for *Soul & Spirit* magazine. Her products are available in most languages worldwide, on Kindle and other eBook platforms, and as iTunes apps.

You can listen to Doreen's live weekly radio show, and call her for a reading, by visiting HayHouseRadio .com®.

www.angeltherapy.com

ABOUT THE AUTHORS

 **Melissa Virtue** began studying dreams and communicating with the angels at a young age. She is an Angel Therapy Practitioner®, a medium and a Light Resonance Healing® Practitioner. Melissa teaches workshops on dream interpretation and angels; created and teaches SpiralDance®, a spiritually based dance technique; and is the author of *Dreamtime* and the children's book series *Magical Dream Journeys*.

www.sacredsolas.com

Hay House Titles of Related Interest

YOU CAN HEAL YOUR LIFE, the movie,
starring Louise Hay & Friends (available as a 1-DVD
programme and an expanded 2-DVD set)
Watch the trailer at: www.LouiseHayMovie.com

THE SHIFT, the movie, starring Dr Wayne W. Dyer
(available as a 1-DVD programme and an expanded 2-DVD set)
Watch the trailer at: www.DyerMovie.com

• ★ •

*COURAGEOUS DREAMING: How Shamans Dream
the World into Being,* by Alberto Villoldo PhD

*DREAMS OF AWAKENING: Lucid Dreaming and Mindfulness of
Dream and Sleep,* by Charlie Morley

THE GOOD NIGHT SLEEP KIT, by Deepak Chopra MD

*THE HIDDEN POWER OF DREAMS: The Mysterious World
of Dreams Revealed,* by Denise Linn

*THE NUMEROLOGY GUIDEBOOK: Uncover Your Destiny
and the Blueprint of Your Life,* by Michelle Buchanan

POWER WORDS: Igniting Your Life with Lightning Force,
by Sharon Anne Klingler

*THE TOP 100 DREAMS: The Dreams That We All Have and What
They Really Mean,* by Ian Wallace

All of the above are available at your local bookstore,
or may be ordered by contacting Hay House
(see next page).

• ★ •

We hope you enjoyed this Hay House book. If you'd like to receive our online catalogue featuring additional information on Hay House books and products, or if you'd like to find out more about the Hay Foundation, please contact:

Hay House UK, Ltd.
Astley House, 33 Notting Hill Gate
London W11 3JQ
Phone: 0-20-3675-2450 • *Fax:* 0-20-3675-2451
www.hayhouse.co.uk • www.hayfoundation.org

∗ ★ ∗

Published and distributed in the United States by:
Hay House, Inc., P.O. Box 5100, Carlsbad, CA 92018-5100
Phone: (760) 431-7695 or (800) 654-5126
Fax: (760) 431-6948 or (800) 650-5115
www.hayhouse.com®

Published and distributed in Australia by: Hay House Australia Pty.
Ltd., 18/36 Ralph St., Alexandria NSW 2015 • *Phone:* 612-9669-4299
Fax: 612-9669-4144 • www.hayhouse.com.au

Published and distributed in the Republic of South Africa by:
Hay House SA (Pty), Ltd., P.O. Box 990, Witkoppen 2068
Phone/Fax: 27-11-467-8904 • www.hayhouse.co.za

Published in India by: Hay House Publishers India, Muskaan
Complex, Plot No. 3, B-2, Vasant Kunj, New Delhi 110 070
Phone: 91-11-4176-1620 • *Fax:* 91-11-4176-1630 • www.hayhouse.co.in

Distributed in Canada by: Raincoast Books, 2440 Viking Way,
Richmond, B.C. V6V 1N2 • *Phone:* 1-800-663-5714
Fax: 1-800-565-3770 • www.raincoast.com

∗ ★ ∗

Take Your Soul on a Vacation

Visit www.HealYourLife.com® to regroup, recharge, and reconnect with your own magnificence. Featuring blogs, mind-body-spirit news, and life-changing wisdom from Louise Hay and friends.

Visit www.HealYourLife.com today!